We Save Wildlife

We Save Wildlife

Les Stocker

with a Foreword by Bill Oddie

WHITTET BOOKS

First published 1986
© 1986 by Les Stocker
Whittet Books Ltd, 18 Anley Road, London W14 OBY

Design by Paul Minns

British Library Cataloguing in Publication Data

Stocker, Les
  We Save Wildlife
  1. Wildlife conservation—Great Britain
  2. Vertebrates—Great Britain
  I. Title
  639.9′76′0941   QL84.4.G7

  ISBN 0–90548–346–4

Printed in Great Britain at The Bath Press, Avon

The author and publisher gratefully acknowledge permission to reprint photographs that appear on the following pages: Bucks and Herts Newspapers, p. 20, p. 42, p. 46, p. 51, p. 55, p. 57, p. 60, p. 68, p. 69, p. 70, p. 72, p. 78, p. 101, p. 105, p. 121 (Barry Keen); *Daily Mirror* (Arthur Sidey), p. 36, p. 126; *Echo and Post*, p. 96; Russell Kilshaw, p. 30; *The Times*, p. 115.

Contents

FOREWORD

Before you – orl – go any further: if you're glancing at this page wondering whether or not to buy the book . . . Do! You'll love it. OK? Good.

Now . . . on with the Foreword.

A visit to Les and Sue Stocker's Wildlife Hospital is an almost surreal experience. Their directions take you through suburban Aylesbury to a house that on the outside looks like a perfectly normal 'detached' – rather like one of those featured in commercials for central heating that have the ideal temperatures super-imposed over each window. You know . . . '60 degrees in the bedroom, 70 degrees in the living room', etc. Pass through the front door ('65 degrees in the hall') and it still looks *fairly* normal, except that the 'hat stand' might well be a live heron. As you carry on into the sitting room take care NOT to wipe your feet on the rabbit skin rug – because the rabbit's still in it! – and make sure that cosy cushion you're about to sit on isn't a snoozing badger. If you have a weak heart don't risk the sofa – heaven knows what might pop up from behind it. It's safer to stay standing, keeping one eye on your scone, which is being nibbled by a three-legged deer, and trying not to let the other eye stare at the curious tatty grey toupée Les seems to be wearing. It's not, in fact, a wig, it's a squirrel.

'Is THIS the hospital?' you ask the squirrel. In this context it seems reasonable to assume that the animals can all talk. It's a bit of a let down when Les or Sue replies instead: 'No – it's out in the garden. This way. Mind the Muntjac!' So outside you go, and, sure enough, there in a tiny suburban Buckinghamshire backyard is a rustic wooden building labelled 'St Tiggywinkle's'! No doubt it's full of hedghogs all wearing spotted headscarves and carrying shopping baskets. Oh, come on! They can't be serious! Can they?

Oh yes, they can . . . And yes, they are – very serious indeed. The fact is this IS a REAL hospital. A hospital for animals; and they're REAL animals. The badgers *don't* wear frock coats, and the squirrels don't talk, in fact if a squirrel open its mouth you'd better keep clear – it's likely to gnaw your finger off! These are WILD animals. Once the visitor realizes this, his or her response changes from bewilderment and amusement to a feeling of tremendous privilege to be allowed so close to foxes, owls, kestrels, sparrowhawks, and how undeniably moving it is to witness the trust and mutual respect between these wild patients and their 'doctors' – Les and Sue Stocker. It's hard not to feel 'sentimental' too, but as you tour the 'wards' – the cages and pens – you cannot fail to appreciate the extraordinary thoroughness and expertise required to care for sick animals. Here creatures will be cured by 'science' not sentiment. Here is gentleness and caring, yes, but, above all, there is immense knowledge.

It is all in this book. Read it and you'll learn a lot, laugh quite a bit, and, I'm pretty sure, cry a little too. The Wildlife Hospital has one paramount purpose: to return the animals back to where they belong – the wild. A few don't make it. Many more do. They *can't* talk, but if they could there's not much doubt what they'd say – 'THANKS' . . .

November 1985   *Bill Oddie*

INTRODUCTION

In 1978, when I started taking in sick and injured wild animals and birds, I never dreamt that there would be so many creatures that needed looking after. The steady stream of casualties brought to our door soon became a flood; it seemed as though we were providing a very much needed service.

Our typically neat suburban garden in Aylesbury, which housed the pens and aviaries, seemed to get smaller yet our overdraft grew larger. Eventually, there was no alternative to forming a registered charity in order to raise funds to support our ever growing number of dependants. Eventually, after a year with over 2,000 admittances, the Wildlife Hospitals Trust was formed in 1983.

By 1985 we were catering for 4,000 casualties each year, still in the confines of our garden. Our intention has always been to return recuperated patients to the wild and thankfully, as most of our intake are released after a short stay, there is always room for more; but we are now running a fund-raising appeal to erect a purpose-built hospital on a more spacious site.

A small band of hard-working volunteers helps us with the hospital work as do our local vets Tuckett, Gray and Partners. Their surgical expertise has proved invaluable over the years especially as many of our cases are new to veterinary science.

Incredibly, Aylesbury, once famous for its ducks, is now becoming more well known for its wildlife hospital and Britain's first hedgehog unit, St Tiggywinkle's, which Susan Hampshire opened for us in 1985.

Each patient arriving at the hospital is an individual – I could tell you hundreds of stories of imperious thrushes, obstinate hares and comical puffins, but working in the confines of this book I have related just a few. They were all characters that will remain vivid in my mind for many years to come. So I hope that next time you come across an injured bird or animal you will think of its possible chances of survival, not just put it out of its misery.

November 1985   *Les Stocker*

1

Purdie

Back in the 1950s, as I grew up in South London, the thought of seeing a bird of prey, especially a kestrel, was my boyhood dream. Every Saturday I would take the number 168 bus out to Wimbledon Common, the wildest place I had ever known. In my wilderness there were woodpeckers, long-tailed tits, nuthatches and in those days every other holly bush housed the nest of a blackbird or the mud-lined construction of a song thrush, but never once did I ever spot a kestrel. I lived in Battersea where there were not even blackbirds, only pigeons and sparrows, and spent many fruitless hours trying to save the lives of these grubby 'townies' as they were injured attempting to survive the dirt and smog of the big city.

As I left school and went to work in an office I had even less time to think about these birds but often wondered, as I sped past them in the commuter race, why they did not fly from the city to a far more pleasing existence in the country. I supposed they were like me and relied on London for everything but somehow I always had this hankering to one day leave the rat race and live in the country, whilst I must admit that I dreaded the hardship of leaving 'civilization'. When eventually I did up and move to Aylesbury it took me two years to finally realize that life could exist outside London; there was a new freedom to travel along unchoked roads. On the other hand it was on these very roads that I started to find many, many birds injured by hit and run drivers. I always stopped and picked them up but they inevitably died, nobody seemed to know how to look after them. The roads were littered with crushed rooks, blackbirds, pigeons, squirrels and then on one memorable day a dead kestrel stared sightless up at me. I had to do something to stop the slaughter.

Purdie would climb to the highest perch.

We Save Wildlife

I scoured every library, bookshop and animal welfare group trying to collect at least a modicum of knowledge. There were a few books but even their information appeared inadequate when faced with an injured bird. Then one day I heard that a captive kestrel was to be destroyed because the owner could no longer maintain it. I could not resist; in no time at all I had driven to Oxford and presented myself to the owner – thankfully in time to prevent the bird's needless demise. He was obviously attached to the bird and I think relieved that I was willing to take on its responsibility and could possibly get it returned to the wild.

Never having handled a bird of prey before that moment, I followed precisely each instruction I had gleaned from all that reading; with thick leather gauntlets I nearly smothered the bird as I tied her into a dark travelling box. She glared up at me, a giant above her; that look from her large dark brown eyes endeared me for ever to the magic of a kestrel; little did I realize that over the years I would come to know hundreds of broken kestrels all with that crystal-clear look of defiant trust that set them apart from other birds. I never believe that any animal casualty realizes that you are trying to help it but somehow kestrels sit still as though accepting assistance, always looking up into your face; it almost seems that they do know.

Back at home with our first kestrel, we were all somewhat in a quandary as to how to remove her from the box; after all inside there was a fearsome bird of prey armed with a vicious flesh-tearing beak and death-dealing needle-sharp talons; it did not seem to matter that she weighed a mere six ounces, she was quite a formidable lady. While we deliberated our approach, my young son Colin insisted that we name her Purdie after the fearless heroine of the television series the Avengers.

The only answer appeared to be to don those enormous gauntlets, in which I could not even bend my fingers, and to open the box parrying any onslaught from the bird. Yet as I opened the top there was no flurry of feathers, beak and talons; instead Purdie just sat there looking up at me. Where was the vicious epitome of everything wild? This kestrel was tamer than most budgerigars: as I put my gloved hand into the box she obligingly stepped onto it. As I lifted

Purdie clear of the box, her predicament struck me: could I possibly release this bird into the wild? She could not hope to hunt the quicksilver mice and voles that she would need to survive on. Considering her future from then on I would have to make a commitment to her for at least another twelve years on the basis of the oldest known kestrel being over sixteen years of age.

Continuing my naive following of the book's instructions I had set up a 'screen perch' in the shed where she was supposed to spend most of her time. She seemed to like the perch; lifting one leg into the warm feathers of her underbelly apparently showed she was relaxed and as she stood there motionless I had the opportunity to marvel at this superb creature. Her feathers, though ruffled and in some cases broken and torn, went through the various subtle shades of brown with dark speckled stripes down her chest and wings and bold black bars across her tail. Her feet and nares (nostrils) were brilliant yellow, contrasting with the black 'moustachial stripe' under each eye, so typical of all the falcons (the stripe serves to reduce the glare of the sun when hunting). The equipment of the falcon was terrifyingly efficient: each foot was armed with four needle-sharp talons for taking and killing prey while the hooked beak, with its characteristic notch on each side, was for tearing at its victims. Her large dark eyes missed nothing; her instant attention was drawn to the slightest movement, even focusing on the minute spiders as they scuttled for cover in the shed roof. It is said that a falcon can identify the small print of *The Times* at a distance of over a mile, and I know that during the time she has been with me Purdie has often spotted some high-flying bird of prey that has been totally outside the scope of my eyesight. She cocks her head to one side and glares skyward, often screaming in alarm, but thankfully the peace is only shattered when other raptors or, for some reason, light aircraft pass overhead.

Her overall appearance was bland compared with a colourful male kestrel but, as with all female birds, it is important that their subdued plumage camouflages them when they are brooding eggs or young in an exposed nest site. To me she was the most glorious creature I had ever seen, what a sacrilege it was to obey those books and keep one of the finest flying birds cooped up in a shed. She might not ever be able to astound motorists with her hovering over the M1 but at least I could give her some space in which she could enjoy her flying prowess; I decided she needed an aviary and as soon as possible.

I set to and built the aviary nine feet long by six feet wide and six feet high, the most I imagined my modest garden would take; little did I know that a few years later there would be fourteen aviaries in that garden taking up nearly forty per cent of the ground area. I knew an old wood nearby where I had spent many hours photographing the fungi on the dead trees. Here I managed to find four long thick branches which Purdie could use for flying between and a nice chunky three-foot-high stump that she could use as a 'plucking post'. The variety in the thicknesses would make her flex her feet and prevent her suffering from bumblefoot, the scourge of captive hawks, wherein the sharp talon on the hind toe penetrates the ball of the foot, causing one of the most persistent, painful infections any bird can suffer. A box with a half-closed front would provide shelter if she required it and a large shallow water dish would serve as a bath. Birds of prey very seldom drink but regularly bathe to keep their plumage in perfect condition.

I felt better as I cut the falconry bell and straps from her legs and released her into the new home but she had never had this much freedom and, somehow bemused, climbed the wiremesh like a parrot. Perhaps she had never had a chance to fly before. She quickly adjusted to the open air and would climb to the highest perch, staying there for hours, flapping those unused wings as if frightened to let go with her feet, then half by accident and half by intention she tumbled forward, let go and made her first flight to the other perch gripping it in a desperate bid to hold on. Her second flight was more successful and soon, with a new-found confidence, she was rocketing from perch to perch, to the ground and then up again. It's often said that birds take the ability to fly for granted but Purdie, on that first day, was obviously revelling in it, thoroughly enjoying every minute of her newly found expertise even in the confines of an aviary. She never made use of the shelter I made her, preferring to sit out in all weathers, not even retreating from the snow the following winter.

From then on I resisted the temptation to handle her so that she could lead as natural an existence as possible. She quickly took to shying away from me if I entered her aviary but she has always maintained her habit of coming to me at the wire to take a titbit before each feeding time.

By this time people in the neighbourhood had heard that I kept a potentially wild bird and gradually started to bring me any injured birds they found; there were the inevitable fledglings ravaged by cats, the courting blackbirds that always seemed to fly low suicide missions in front of cars, the crows, pigeons and rooks cruelly shot in the wing and then, the first summer Purdie was with me, an extremely colourful male kestrel that had been found flightless in the middle of a meadow. Most of our casualties can be directly attributed to the close proximity of man but any accidents of nature always seem to remain a mystery. This male kestrel had somehow lost all the primary feathers off his right wing. How this happened we shall never know, but I knew that he would have to stay with us until he grew a replacement set. Unlike ducks and some other birds that moult their flight feathers all at one time, birds of prey, in order to stay fully capable of hunting, only shed two feathers at a time, one from each wing. Sometimes I have had to keep a kestrel for over a year in order that all its feathers are renewed and perfect. However, if a feather is plucked its replacement starts growing straight away so hopefully this male would not be with us for long. As it was I only had two aviaries by then, and one had small garden birds in it, so he would have to share with Purdie.

Luckily I had gained some relevant information from all those books: male falcons are at least one third smaller than females, hence their title of 'tiercels' and a female was unlikely to accept a strange male into her domain. The only way to get both birds into the aviary was to remove Purdie for two weeks and contain her in a new aviary while the male established his territory unmolested by her. Purdie was somewhat aggressive when we returned her two weeks later but I think she was only asserting her dominance in the 'pecking order'. She would always take first choice of the food I offered but I had to make sure that there was enough for the male.

We Save Wildlife

All through that summer, then autumn, there was no improvement in the male's wing; he did grow some primary feathers but they were stunted and only half the length they should have been. The birds' female-dominated co-existence continued peaceably until the following March when suddenly both of them started screeching at each other. As a kestrel's scream is an ear-shattering experience we could not help but notice their new interest in each other where previously there had been apathy.

Watching them closely I noticed that Purdie had stopped flying down for her food; she was now staying on the highest perch as though screaming her instructions to the male to bring her food. Surprisingly he started to oblige, flying up to the perch and, shuffling towards her with dead mice dangling from his beak, he would stretch forward so that she could take the offering. Could this be the classic food-passing that forges a bond between birds just prior to copulation? For days we watched from the kitchen window as they became more and more excited and Purdie more and more demanding until finally everything must have been to her liking as she allowed a very noisy mating to take place. This ritual carried on many times every day for the following two weeks until on the morning of April 23rd Purdie was missing from her usual post on the highest perch.

Although I did not want to disturb their arrangements, I just had to know the outcome of that two weeks of torrid activity. Donning my lightweight leather gloves, I ventured into the aviary and, much to the defiant consternation of the male bird, reached into the box. Purdie was sitting on the pile of pellets that served as a nest, and I gently lifted her clear. Thankfully I had those leather gloves on as she did everything in her power to tear them to shreds but, undaunted and with her screaming from my left hand, I peered in to see three heavily blotched eggs, each about one and a half inches long. I had disturbed the birds enough so hastily withdrew from the aviary, leaving Purdie to return to her charges. Assuming that she had laid the three eggs on alternate days, she must have started laying four days before, on April 19th, but their development would not start until she started brooding in earnest – probably today, the 23rd. Kestrels usually incubate their eggs for twenty-eight days so we would have to wait and see if all their endeavours were fruitful. In the meantime Purdie was a model parent, only ever leaving the nest when she was hungry and even then the male was instructed to take her place.

It appeared that nobody had ever monitored the growth of kestrel chicks so if the eggs did hatch here was a golden opportunity to record their progress and provide a comparison for use with any orphans brought to the hospital in the future. Working with Philip Burton, I could individually mark any hatchlings with felt-tip pen then each day could weigh, photograph and record their growth. We could also take occasional measurements of the increase in size of their primary feathers, bills, leg bones and wing lengths. All we needed now was for the eggs to hatch. It certainly seemed to take more than four weeks to reach D-Day, May 21st.

The great day eventually arrived and as early as possible I once again donned my leather gloves and with a camera hold-all slung round my neck, made my approach to the nest box. Purdie as usual flew out to waylay me; talons thrust forward, she locked on to my gloved hand giving me the opportunity to cast off my other glove and feel inside the box. Groping in the dark I felt the warm smoothness of incubating eggs but then a tiny fluffy but very bony chick. When I lifted it out I was confronted with a minute ball of blue/white down with ridiculously large and uncontrollable pale pink feet and legs. Putting it carefully into the hold-all I once more reached into the box and withdrew another chick and then another; three eggs had in fact hatched and I could still feel another three.

Quickly I released Purdie into her box and rushed with the youngsters into the kitchen where I had laid out all the measuring and recording equipment. First I marked each chick with blue felt-tip pen: the eldest had the ignominy of a large blue spot on its rump, the second chick had its spot underneath while number three was marked under its right wing. I quickly weighed them on a Pesola precision spring-balance; the eldest weighed in at 16 grams, the second at $15\frac{1}{2}$ grams and number three a massive $16\frac{1}{2}$ grams. A quick photograph, then without further delay I once again had to endure Purdie's anger and was relieved to see her join them once more in the

On the fifth day the chicks opened their eyes.

box. Luckily birds have little if any sense of smell so there was no danger of my scent being detected on the chicks.

The following day saw the hatching of 'blue spot on the head' at $16\frac{1}{2}$ grams and the day after 'blue spot under left wing' and 'no spots' at $15\frac{3}{4}$ grams and 16 grams respectively.

Every day after then I collected up all six chicks and recorded their phenomenal growth. On the fifth day they opened their eyes and by the ninth day each had gained over 100 grams in weight. Their egg teeth (used to break out of the egg) on the end of their bills disappeared about 11 days after hatching and their feathers started to show through, each inside its own little sheath. In only another 13 days the eldest chick, 'blue spot on rump', had all its feathers with just some down still remaining on its crown and the nape of its neck. By the time I stopped recording them, 29 days after hatching, they were difficult to tell from adult birds and were taking their first

The eldest chick had most of its feathers.

precarious flights around the aviary. They were still extricating food from the two overworked adults but gradually mastered the art of tearing meat for themselves.

In the wild kestrels are independent of their parents at 13 weeks after hatching but I decided to give these six a further 3 weeks just to make sure they had as much experience as possible before release. We had ringed them in order to monitor their progress so at 16 weeks

Purdie and her mate have raised chicks again this year.

I released them all directly from their home aviary. This would ensure that if they still needed feeding they would be able to return to the fold. One did stay around for some weeks but soon joined the others in dispersing throughout the country.

From then on we viewed every kestrel brought to us with apprehension but none of them was ever brought back to us. As far as we know they all survived in the wild, excepting one that was found six months later stuck in a factory chimney in Essex a considerable distance from its birthplace.

There is very little chance of a naturally wild kestrel surviving its first year so we feel fairly sure that the five remaining of Purdie's chicks have done remarkably well.

Purdie and her mate soon forgot the six young kestrels and settled

The chicks were difficult to tell from the adult birds.

down to a winter of domestic bliss. Both birds are still with us: Purdie unable to be released because of her tameness and the male who still has not grown a set of primary feathers that would enable him to fly properly. They have raised chicks again this year and even took on the responsibility of three orphan kestrels, bringing up to release a total of eight youngsters, which must be a record for a bird of prey. The eight will be going soon and once again we shall have to wait and see if this male grows a decent set of primaries.

I now have to treat many kestrels each year, a far cry from those fruitless days back in London but at least the grubby sparrows and pigeons are still arriving and happily we are managing to keep them alive and release them in the wide open freshness of Buckingham-shire.

2

Badgers of the Road

Before Sue and I committed our lives to tending sick and injured wildlife we spent many years preparing ourselves for the venture. We avidly consumed every book we could find on the subject of animal welfare and travelled the country to meet people who had experience of the type of casualties we were likely to encounter. The late John Hughes was a champion of wildlife casualties with an unparalleled knowledge acquired over twenty-five years of caring for every type of animal and bird. In our early days his willingness to advise helped us through some of the heartbreaking situations that arise when caring for injured creatures. In particular he warned of the terrible consequences of vehicles hitting badgers as they followed centuries-old trackways that had been intersected by modern highways. Usually the victims did not appear badly injured but spinal and internal injuries which can be fatal do not always show; even John could only save one badger out of every five involved in accidents. The main problem appears to be that badgers will not flee an approaching car as other animals do, instead they turn to face the aggressor, heads down and resolved not to give way until the inevitable collision takes place.

We accepted that we would be up against an exceptionally high mortality rate but we were not aware that most badger casualties were being humanely destroyed before we could even reach the scenes of accidents to assess the victim's injuries. Naturally any animals, including dogs and cats, that have been involved in road traffic accidents will suffer some pain and may well turn to bite would-be rescuers. Badgers will behave like this and, as their bites can easily amputate fingers, many people do not want to handle casualties, preferring to destroy them on the spot. I was quite prepared to handle badger casualties and had strong animal graspers and cages on stand-by but somehow others always appeared to reach the animals before us. It took months of cajoling and publicity before the badger calls started to come in, and we embarked on our project to challenge that eighty per cent mortality rate.

The first call came in: a badger had apparently been hit by a car on the main Oxford to Aylesbury road and had somehow dragged itself up the driveway of an adjacent cottage where it was now lying outside the garage doors. It was seven o'clock on a wet and windy March morning but the weather did not seem to be important. We had been ready for this moment for months, so the grasper, cage and blankets were thrown in the car and within minutes we had covered the five miles to the scene of the accident. We could see the badger, just a black and grey heap by the garage door, so I stopped at the end of the drive, intending to proceed on foot. With grasper poised to prevent its premature dash to a doubtful freedom, I crept towards the badger; its small size suggested that it was a female, a sow. As I approached her she showed no sign of movement, yet I was still very cautious as I knew that badgers could spring from harmless inertia to snapping ferocity in an instant. Tentatively I touched her with the tip of the grasper. Nothing. Prodded her a little harder. Still nothing. Reaching down, I was ready to catch hold of her scruff but as I did so I realized that she was dead, now only another statistic confirming that eighty per cent.

At the time the controversy about badgers supposedly spreading bovine tuberculosis was raging and we felt it our duty to have an autopsy carried out by the Ministry of Agriculture. The local Ministry vet cleared the badger of any disease and also told us that all the sixty-three road casualty corpses autopsied that year had been healthy. It was heartening that there was no tuberculosis in the area but that figure of sixty-three more road accident corpses really hit home.

The following week Charlie Norris, our local RSPCA Inspector, called me out to a live badger that had been spotted inside a garden shed at Marsworth, not far from Aylesbury. The house dog had been whining at the shed door and on investigation the householder had been met by a very subdued badger half-hidden under some old sacks. Entering the very dark shed, we could see no sign of the badger, it had made its way to the farthest, blackest corner under even more piles of old sacks. Gingerly we lifted the sacks and other rubbish until we could slip the grasper over the badger's head. A badger's neck is so thick and powerful that I always slide the grasper over one front leg as well, and this makes sure that it cannot slip off over the animal's head. There was obviously something very wrong with this badger for, as I lifted her clear of the sacks, there was no fight, no struggle whatsoever. Outside, in the daylight we shuddered at the extent of her appalling injuries; we can only marvel at how she had managed to drag herself from the road to the solace of that shed. Together with our vets we try to treat all manner of injuries but obvious head and brain damage is beyond repair. There is no cure. Sadly we had no alternative other than to put her painlessly to sleep. On the journey back to Aylesbury neither of us uttered a word, we knew that we were both having those guilty, nagging doubts that plague you after you have prematurely ended an animal's life. Was there an alternative? Should we have waited? Were the injuries not really that serious? In reality we had no option; if the badger had lived it would have suffered immense pain before finally succumbing. It had to be done.

The next badger casualty arrived at three o'clock in the morning. One of the vets, Robin, had been called out to the scene of the accident and had decided to bring the female straight to us so that we could start recuperative care immediately. She was a small female and as her rear legs were not moving we conjectured that the car had caught her across the back. She laid there motionless; our great fear was that her spinal cord had been damaged, but by pinching her back feet with forceps we could feel a reaction, and she had in fact fractured her pelvis. Her back legs were splayed out so I could easily see that her paws were soft and fleshy with five forward-pointing toes so reminiscent of a human hand. It's amazing to think that badgers can scrabble in the roughest terrain without any harm coming to these soft 'hands'.

Robin had considerable experience of dogs and cats suffering fractured pelvises and recommended that Mealy be closely confined for six weeks. I had built a unit specifically to house badgers with this type of injury so after Robin had administered some glucose and saline, to counteract her shock and dehydration, we laid Mealy on a bed of fresh hay and put bowls of dog food and water within easy reach of her head.

Mealy declined to eat or drink for the first few days and consequently had to suffer four-hourly injections of glucose and saline to combat her low fluid and sugar levels. Although the injections were painless, she always cowered at our approach, covering her head with her front paws; she obviously did not understand that we were not responsible for the ache in her back legs.

Gradually she trusted us more and did start to feed, but we were worried, she looked so dull and listless, quite unlike a recuperating wild animal.

Then one morning she was dead, free of pain and the strange world she had been subjected to. The post mortem revealed that Mealy's liver had been damaged in the accident, an injury that could not have been rectified by any amount of surgery.

Another death to add to the grim toll of road casualty statistics. Our success rate stood at nil, even worse than the eighty per cent.

One morbid trend emerging was that all our road casualties so far had been sows, reminding us of our experiences with frogs and toads on their spring migrations when most of the flattened corpses on the road appeared to be spawn-carrying females. True to form the next badger casualty was a sow, brought ignominiously to the hospital in the boot of a car. Luckily for the driver the badger was unconscious and unable to put up a fight. We are always worried that an inert animal may revive during a car journey and turn on its rescuer.

I laid her out on the surgery table to check her for injuries or abrasions. Happily everything seemed intact although she was obviously suffering from severe concussion. I gave her injections of glucose and saline then made her comfortable on a bed of hay under an infra-red lamp to maintain her temperature while she was still in a shocked and comatose condition. I sat with her for over an hour, since she would either die from her head injury or else gradually wake up. She started to move, her eyes flickered open, she looked

26

quite drunk but was I relieved at these signs of life. Her eyes were not focused and trembled incessantly with a condition known as 'nystagmus' typical of concussive injuries to the head. Although badgers' eyes are very small and not very efficient, their powers of smell and hearing are phenomenal. I knew that even if she could not see us she would be able to tell from our movements exactly where we were. Her revival meant that we would now have to handle her with the utmost care and respect.

For days she showed little interest in life; she behaved very like Mealy had done. Surely she could not be dying from an unknown internal injury? After six days, she came to life, shuffling her bedding around in true badger fashion, making herself as comfortable as she could. She started to act like a badger, sleeping on her back with her feet in the air, oblivious to all those peering in to catch a glimpse of her. She slept through everything, we just had to call her Dormy.

Dormy looked bright enough when she condescended to wake up, but she would not feed. I realize that badgers can semi-hibernate without food for some days, especially in periods of extreme cold weather, but it was now over a week since her arrival. I put down different foods to try to tempt her: bread soaked in sweet syrup, meat covered in honey, dog foods, cat foods, I even tried her on roast turkey. Still she showed no interest whatsoever and ten days had elapsed. I dug up fat juicy earthworms, raided the kestrels' larder for frozen day-old chicks; fish – frozen, fried and fingered – was ignored. It was now twelve days and I was contemplating the daunting prospect of force-feeding her with Complan. My last resort was the frozen mice I get in for any owl casualties; I defrosted a dozen and dropped them by her nose so that she could not miss them. The following morning they had gone, so we concluded she had a secret penchant for frozen mice. We were all relieved that she had let us into her secret and thanked goodness for our supply of frozen mice.

After that we could not stop her eating, she ate and slept, ate and slept, never showing much inclination to exert herself in any other way. Two weeks of this halcyon existence interspersed with compulsory exercise and Dormy was ready for release. We knew she had been found near to the village of Worminghall; so we set two of our

We Save Wildlife

voluntary helpers, who lived there, the task of trying to trace the sett where Dormy may have resided. Tracking from the scene of the accident, Paul and Louise found a sett on farmland that ran adjacent to the road. We had to assume that this was Dormy's sett and, with the farmer's complete approval, arranged to release her as soon as possible.

I had to resort to muzzling Dormy with a bandage.

I had not handled Dormy since her arrival in the boot of the car. I was pleased at how strong she was now. I intended to lift her from her pen into a travelling cage for the twelve-mile journey to Worminghall, but had to resort to muzzling her with a bandage. She had become so strong there was a danger that I might not be able to hold her, and the simple bandage muzzle protected me if that were to

I had to wade across a stream before Dormy could be released.

happen. Also I knew that at Worminghall I would have to carry her across some rough terrain to reach the sett, and I could not take the chance of being bitten.

At Worminghall Dormy seemed to sense familiar surroundings, which was as much a relief for me as it must have been for her. She was so keen to go that it took all my strength and concentration to hold her and I now saw that I had to wade across a stream before she could be released. Tucking her under one arm, I tentatively felt my way across until I reached the other bank. The sett seemed to start at the water's edge and as there was no way that I could climb out, I decided to let Dormy go there. She lodged her front claws in the bank, nearly pulling me over as I desperately tried to untie the muzzle. I held on to the loose end as she pulled it off; then she was away, waddling as badgers do, stopping at the top of the bank to look back at me, then she was gone. The whole team had looked on

The tell-tale hairline pinpointed the damage to Big Brock's jaw.

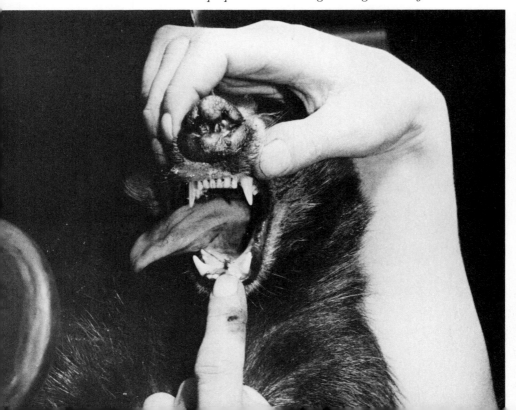

spellbound as she went but now the thrill of seeing her go bubbled over, we had done it, we had won our first battle to get a road casualty badger back into the wild.

Some months passed before our next badger road casualty was brought to the hospital. In the meantime we had released badgers from snares and had raised for release our first badger cub, Biddy.

Big Brock was our next unfortunate road victim; for a change he was a boar badger who was somewhat subdued on arrival, possibly from the sedating effect of a concussion. He had obvious head damage and needed X-rays and further sedation in case he came around. At the vet's he was completely anaesthetized and laid out for X-rays of different parts of his head and snout. There was damage to the small thin bones of his snout but these would heal spontaneously without any added fixation. More worrying was a fracture of his

Big Brock was somewhat subdued on arrival – here he was initially kept in an incubator.

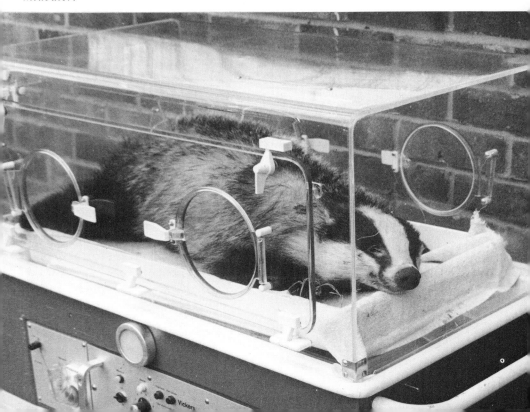

lower jaw which effectively split it completely in half. As he was still unconscious we could safely open his mouth; the tell-tale hairline of blood running from his incisor teeth back along under his tongue pinpointed the damage. We had successfully treated a hedgehog with a similar fracture so the prognosis looked good. Chris Troughton, the vet handling this case, sutured the two jaw halves rigid with special surgical wire. With the mouth open we could also check Brock for damage to those impressive teeth, but they all looked sound and formidable as ever.

With the surgery completed I took full advantage of the remaining anaesthesia and quickly transported Brock back to the badger box in the hospital. A bed of fresh hay and an infra-red lamp made him as comfortable as possible and helped maintain the body temperature so easily lost after an anaesthetic. From now on it was just a matter of feeding him until the wire came out in six weeks' time.

No sooner had I settled him into his box than a call came from a veterinary practice in Leighton Buzzard, about twelve miles north of Aylesbury. They had been treating a sow road casualty for paralysis of her back legs. There was no skeletal injury, it was probably damage to the muscles and tendons of her back that had kept her inactive for about three weeks. Rest and confinement were the most suitable treatment, and they asked if we would take over her care as we had more facilities for keeping adult badgers. Of course we agreed and within the hour Bridget had arrived. She was quite a bit smaller than Brock and a *little* bit friendlier.

We settled her in the badger box at the opposite end to Big Brock, with a partition to keep them apart, but with the proximity of each other's scent to comfort them. She had endured three weeks of captivity so was quite familiar with tinned dog meat and other manufactured foods. However they both relished the frozen mice that had been such a hit with Dormy.

The more natural diet seemed to suit Bridget, and within a week she was moving her back legs and one week later was strong enough to be introduced to her grumpy neighbour. Slowly I lifted the partition but neither of them showed the slightest interest in the other. I sat by the box for two hours before Brock made his move towards Bridget; I was prepared for the possibility of an attack on her but I was very wrong in my assumption that he was aggressive to everything. He sniffed her, she sniffed back and before very long they were coiled in a knot seemingly more than content with each other's company. From that moment on Brock looked after Bridget, always sleeping on the outside, growling and shaking menacingly every time I approached.

I hated keeping them in that box but had no alternative until at last, three weeks later, Bridget had recovered sufficiently to be put into an outside pen. We decided to make use of the impregnability of the squirrel pen which was surrounded by a large paved area that would be impregnable to a badger's digging. Two tea chests filled with fresh hay provided weatherproof shelter, so using the grasper I transferred the now very strong badgers to their new home. It took all my strength to hold Big Brock in the grasper. Bridget was easier to handle but in the following week even she escaped the grasp of one of our voluntary helpers and nearly succeeded in clamping those jaws on his unwary hand. He was lucky to escape with just a graze. This closest of shaves prompted me to insist that in future I would be the only person allowed to handle adult badgers.

Bridget followed Brock into one of the cosy tea chests and with a great deal of rustling and banging they sorted the bedding to their liking. We did not see any sign of them for three days. The food I put out was left untouched. I knew that badgers lie low after a disturbance, but thought they should have settled by now. I did not realize just how well they had settled, for after the fourth night I was greeted by an enormous pile of earth, a gaping hole and no badgers; but at least the food had been taken. The hole disappeared under the tea chests and, judging by the amount of soil displaced in one night, it would not be long before the two badgers were beyond my reach. As they both still needed medical attention I had no alternative but to dig them out.

Being over-cautious I decided to keep everybody else out of the pen and to carry out the extraction on my own. Feeling down the hole with a stick brought forth no sign of the badgers but by judging the general direction of the excavation I could prod through the soil until I felt the soft resistance of a badger at least two feet below the surface. Needless to say, it was raining and so, covered in mud, I toiled for most of the day until at last the first few black and grey hairs appeared. I did not want to injure the animals so I had to clear the remaining soil with my bare hands. Bridget was the first badger I managed to extricate from the new hole; it was a simple job to put the grasper over her head and lift her into a temporary tea chest. Big Brock had other ideas, and my first knowledge of his whereabouts were four gleaming canine teeth growling at me from the darkness. As I presented the grasper he clamped onto the steel-reinforced leather strap and, although it gave me the opportunity to inspect his once broken jaw, there was no way he would let me slide the grasper over his head. I removed some more soil but my next approach brought the same rebuff, with the grasper suffering another attack from those jaws. We carried on like this for some time, with me never once getting the grasper over his head until the last time he clamped on to it and would not let go; as if to show the power of his repaired bottom jaw, he held onto the grasper until I had pulled him clear of the hole. Quickly I grabbed his rump and dumped him unceremoniously in the other tea chest.

Housing them in a squirrel pen had obviously not been a good idea and I now needed to cover the floor of it with chain-link fencing. Levelling all my excavations, I laid the chain-link and dressed it with a fresh layer of turf so that the pen looked as good as new. Once again the hay-filled tea chests were offered as quarters and the two badgers released. I went to bed that night exhausted but satisfied that the pen was secure. Again another three days elapsed before the food was taken and on the fourth morning there was the gaping hole with no sign of the badgers.

This time I had no alternative; after another day's digging Brock and Bridget had to be returned to their original badger box. The sooner they were released into the wild the sooner I would not have this constant battle to keep them confined.

Big Brock still had the wire through his jaw. This had to be removed before he could be released and as we wanted them to go together I had to arrange a visit to the vet's for the simple task of taking the wire out. Did I say simple task? Brock had other ideas. I managed to get him into a travelling cage but at the vet's I could not pull him out, he lodged his feet obstinately inside the edge of the cage and would not move. He would need sedating before the wire could be removed so while I engaged him in another extrication battle, Richard, another of our vets, deftly injected a dose of ACP, a very efficient sedative. Did I say very efficient? Once again Brock had other ideas and even a half hour later he was still resisting my attempts to get him out.

Eventually, at grasper's length, I had him free, so gripping his rump with my free hand I carried him, wriggling like a giant eel, into the surgery. Richard managed, at the third attempt, to get a bandage muzzle around Brock's jaws but it still took two of us to hold the badger while Richard snipped and with one pull removed the wire. A hasty retreat to the car and once again Big Brock was safely in the travelling cage.

Back at the hospital I only had to put the cage entrance next to the badger box and Brock was once more back with Bridget.

The next question was where to release the pair of them; they had been in captivity so long that they would be liable to attack from other badgers if we released them without picking the site very carefully. Also it was very difficult to find an unused sett that we could guarantee was vacant. The only alternative was to build them a sett on a bank of land well away from other setts and roads but in a situation where badger-baiters would not be able to persecute them.

We found an ideal situation inside a five-hundred-year-old hedge that had not been trimmed for centuries. In the centre of an 800-acre farm there was little fear of disturbance or danger from traffic and, once settled, they would be able to find all the food they could ever need. With a squad of five other men we set to, on a cold Sunday morning, to dig out the sett. We wished we possessed a badger's prowess at digging for no sooner had we broken the surface than we met a nearly impassable bed of flints. With two men pick-axing and the rest shovelling, we managed to dig the main chamber about five feet wide and four feet deep. This would be covered by a solid wooden roof in turn covered with the soil and the flints that we had taken out. Two channels were dug from the chamber with two large diameter concrete pipes serving as entrance and exit. Before it was closed in, the chamber was filled with fresh hay, a spattering of the old bedding from their box at the hospital, a whole bag of defrosted mice and a dozen goose eggs left as a welcoming present to the potential owners.

When the sett was complete and the camouflaged tunnels cleared I drove back to Aylesbury to collect Brock and Bridget.

When I had returned to the sett I removed Brock from his travelling cage, ignominiously at the end of a brand-new grasper. The old grasper had finally given up and the steel wire snapped after his constant onslaught. I offered him to the first tunnel, pulled the quick release and he was gone into the dark sanctuary of his new home. Bridget did not need the grasper so I carried her and sent her up the tunnel to join Brock. There was much rustling in the hay at

Bridget did not need the grasper as I released her into the sett.

the end of the tunnel, I hoped they were settling down.

Over the next few weeks we arranged daily visits to the sett to see if we could spot the tenants, but only the movement of hay and a few holes dug around the entrance tunnel gave us any clue of their presence.

We were then level pegging with statistics, having released fifty per cent of our road casualties, but the motor car had the last word. Only this morning we were told of a badger hit on the road on the other side of the village of Whitchurch. Without hesitation we jumped in the car and sped to Whitchurch, making very good time apart from crawling for a time behind the inevitable tractor, but we arrived to find yet another sow badger stiff and cold. The statistics were fighting a rearguard action but, spurred by our successes, we know that the tide can be turned and more badgers saved, and we haven't given up.

3

Vix's Tale

Our policy at the hospital is to ask people to bring any animal casualties to us, rather than us going to collect them. This procedure allows us to be available for any other callers. It also keeps petrol costs to a minimum and halves the time it takes to get a casualty into care. We do make exceptions for larger, more 'dangerous' animals and birds, priding ourselves on being mobile within minutes of a call. The 'dangerous' animals include deer, swans, badgers, foxes and the larger birds of prey. Swans and badgers will not hesitate to attack; deer can be dangerous purely because of their size, although muntjac bucks have sharp tusks in their upper jaw. These are weapons used in the rut and are often used to deter any would-be captor. Foxes show great fear of being handled and will snap if cornered. They do not have the biting power of the badger but their razor-sharp teeth can cause slashing wounds that are very likely to become infected. Most fox casualties will cower in a corner and defecate with fright, but one young vixen we were called to showed defiance from the moment she was captured and never once accepted her period in captivity.

One day in 1984 a young American serviceman called us to say that there was a fox lying in a field near his home in Bicester. The fox had been there for some time and was obviously very weak. After he had given us directions, we asked that he go back to the field and wait for us. On no account should anybody try to approach an animal for fear of panicking it into a premature flight where we might not find it again.

Loading the grasper, a noose-like affair for catching mammals, a blanket, hot-water bottle and animal-carrying basket, we set off to cover the twenty miles to Bicester as quickly as possible. As always, the journey seemed to take for ever but luckily we found the site immediately so saving a lot of valuable time.

A small crowd had gathered but thankfully nobody had tried to get near to the fox who was still lying in the field. It must have been very weak for normally foxes remain hidden during the day and only stay exposed if unable to reach even the smallest amount of cover. I had to wade a stream and assault a barbed-wire fence before I could reach the field. Taking the grasper in both hands I tentatively started to approach her. In this situation the grasper is essential, as even the most debilitated fox, at the time of imminent capture, will summon up one last ounce of energy and make a dash for cover and can also still manage to turn and snap at any unwary fingers.

The fox looked quite small so I thought that she was probably an immature female (vixen). True to form, at my approach, she did make a forlorn dash for freedom. Her left front leg dragged to one side. I could see that it was severely injured, with all the skin and fur missing. With the hindrance of the damaged leg she kept toppling over so with a desperate dash I managed at the second attempt to slip the padded noose over her head. She turned and glared at me; with ears back and teeth bared, she spat defiance at me spluttering a growl that reminded me of the mountain lions in old Wild West movies. Carefully I used the grasper to pin her to the ground, then with my right hand I took a firm hold of the loose skin at the back of her neck. This 'scruffing' of an animal often causes it to relax completely and hang limp just like a kitten being carried by its mother. However, it's as well to remember to use your strongest hand for the scruffing, leaving your weak hand to support the body weight. Not that this vixen was any trouble to hold but I do remember one sow badger that was brought to the hospital. I foolishly scruffed with her my weaker left hand and very nearly lost control and possibly a couple of fingers.

Taking a quick look at her injuries, I could see the remains of a wire snare around the top of her leg, but as there was no obvious haemorrhage needing urgent attention I decided to get her to the vet's without further delay. Sue, with the carrying basket, had followed me into the field. Gently I lowered Vix, as we called her, onto the fresh towel in the basket. Her leg was obviously very painful, so the smallest movement must have caused her agony. The

39

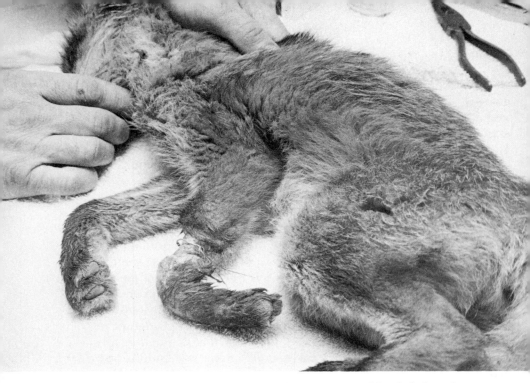

Vix was found with the remains of a snare around her left front leg.

small crowd of onlookers were all very relieved to see that she was alive and many remarked that they had never seen a fox so close and how beautiful she was.

When dealing with a mammal with serious injuries I never administer any medication, other than a dextrose/saline injection (to combat dehydration), until one of the veterinary surgeons has prescribed remedial treatment.

Vix was somewhat dehydrated and needed fluids but we decided to go direct to the vet's so that treatment could begin as soon as possible. We stopped at a call box and telephoned Richard Hill at the hospital. Richard handled many of our mammal casualties and told us to go straight in, he would be standing by to work on the vixen as soon as we arrived.

Each time we pass, with a wild animal, through the waiting room, the people sitting there, with their dogs and cats, always express

40

deep concern for the well-being of our charge. This day was no exception in spite of the fact that their friendly concern was met with spits and snarls from Vix. Knowing that I only needed to take serious cases to the Veterinary Hospital, Richard ushered me direct-ly into the operating theatre where all the necessary equipment was to hand.

Vix was still spitting and snapping, being very unco-operative, so we decided to tie her muzzle with a linen bandage. Dropping a loop over the jaws, pulling it tight and tying it behind the head is a system that has been used for many years, especially for aggressive dogs. With a double loop the system works just as well on badgers and foxes. It causes them no harm but does permit the close inspection and treatment of even the most irascible biter.

With Vix safely muzzled, but still glaring her hate, our first job was to remove the wire snare that we could now see had not cut through to the bone. Not many veterinary practices carry wire-cutting snips but luckily I had a pair in the car's tool box. Pulling the snare out of the torn flesh, I managed to slide the snips under the wire and cut it free.

To clean the damaged leg would have been very painful to her so Richard decided to give her a light anaesthetic. A few minutes later she was asleep so we could get an uninterrupted look at the extent of her injuries. Using a cetrimide disinfectant solution we cleaned the leg, abrasively removing any dirt or dead tissue. Most of the leg was raw, with all the skin and fur having been chafed away by the snare. She had worn three of her toes away by dragging the snare some distance exposing any bones that were still intact. It appeared to me that she had stepped into a rabbit snare attached to a heavy weight and had dragged it for many days before finally collapsing with exhaustion. Wild creatures are at their lowest ebb of life when they can be caught like this, and so urgent treatment is the only hope of saving them.

After the initial cleaning, a final dowsing with Dermisol removed any loose dead tissue and would help regeneration and the growth of new skin. We decided not to cover the cleaned wounds as exposure to the air would encourage faster regeneration. Wrapping her, still

Most of Vix's leg was raw, with all the skin and fur having been chafed away.

unconscious, into a blanket with a hot-water bottle to maintain her body heat, we carried her to the car for the journey back to base.

Sue had gone ahead to deal with any other emergency calls and had also prepared a wire-topped pen about 3ft long by 2ft wide. Vix was starting to come round, so we placed her on a soft blanket in the pen. As she was still semi-conscious an infra-red heater above the pen kept her body heat constant.

By the following morning she was fully awake and greeted me with her repertoire of warning signs and growls. The laid-back ears, grinning teeth and angry snarl told me that she regarded this new home as a prison. I tried to coax her to friendliness but she had her mind set on tearing my hands to shreds. Gingerly I lowered a bowl of dog food into her box. This would be easy for her to eat, for, although a wild fox can go some time between feeds, she had obviously starved for many days so it was imperative that she had some nourishment. I did not relish the thought of force-feeding her and no doubt she would not have taken too kindly to the further indignity.

I left her to it and watched from a discreet distance to see if she showed any interest in the food. It was over an hour before she moved towards it, then, instead of tucking into the proffered feast, she gripped the edge of the feeding bowl, shook it like a rat and scattered Pedigree Chum everywhere. This appeared to be part of her natural routine, for as soon as the bowl was presumably 'dead' she settled down and noisily ate the dog food, all the time scanning with her eyes and ears as though something might deprive her of it.

She finished off three tins of Pedigree Chum on that first day. In the process she scattered food everywhere, her blanket was now a mess and her bad leg liberally spattered with dog food. I was due to give her another antibiotic injection and decided to clean up at the same time. With the help of the grasper I once again scruffed her, lifting her clear of the box. Sue removed the blanket and generally cleaned up any uneaten food. Normally foxes in captivity prefer to have no bedding so, although it seemed harsh, we decided that Vix would stay cleaner without any. In spite of all the stories, we find that foxes are very clean animals and appreciate regular cleaning.

I held Vix while Sue cleaned the leg with Dermisol; more dead tissue came away but it did certainly look much healthier than it had the day before. I administered her daily antibiotic injection into the large muscle of one of her back legs. Intramuscular injections are more quickly effective than subcutaneous injections given under the skin. Once back in her box, Vix voiced her disapproval. We wished she could understand that we were trying to help her.

For the next few days we followed the same routine. Her leg

43

wounds were improving but I became increasingly concerned that she did not appear to be able to straighten the leg. I phoned Richard, and he suggested we take her to the surgery to check the muscles and tendons.

Once again Vix was lightly anaesthetized. Richard had not seen her since that first visit, and he remarked on the noticeable improvement in the flesh wounds. Wild animals have remarkable powers of regeneration, we have had many casualties that show scars from old wounds that would have debilitated any domestic creature. Although her leg had improved there was obviously something not right with the main tendons. They had been damaged by the snare and were now healing in a contracted position that would make it impossible for Vix to flex her leg properly. The only way to prevent a permanent disability was to plaster the leg in an extended position to stretch the tendons and keep them elastic. The worry now was that to cover the leg with plaster was inviting all manner of secondary infection into the open wounds. Unfortunately there was no alternative: we would just have to be doubly vigilant in case something did go amiss. We had to try and keep her as immobile as possible so she would have to stay in her small box for some weeks to come.

Once again we carried her back to the Wildlife Hospital, this time with her plastered leg stuck out in front of her. What would she think when she came round and felt the constriction on her leg? We did not have long to wait: as she became aware of the situation she must have imagined herself back in that snare; she smashed around her box, tearing at the plaster. Nothing quietened her down and we became worried that she might further damage herself with her frenzied tossing and turning.

We had seen dogs and cats with large bucket-like contrivances around their necks. The purpose of these collars was to stop them aggravating a wound or dressed area. How would Vix take to a collar? Would it be yet another snare for her to cope with? Once again there was no alternative, so we adapted a small dog's collar and fitted it to Vix. She obviously did not like it but at least it quietened her and protected that leg from further damage. Then yet another problem came to light – her nose did not reach the front of

44

The only way to prevent a permanent disability was to plaster the leg in an extended position.

the collar, so how was she to eat or drink? The answer proved to be deep Tupperware dishes that allowed her to slide the collar over them so she could reach the contents.

How on earth do you explain to a wild animal, recently freed from a snare, that the plaster around its leg, the collar around its neck and the small box in which it is incarcerated are not just extensions of the original torture and that there will be a time when it will be free? She

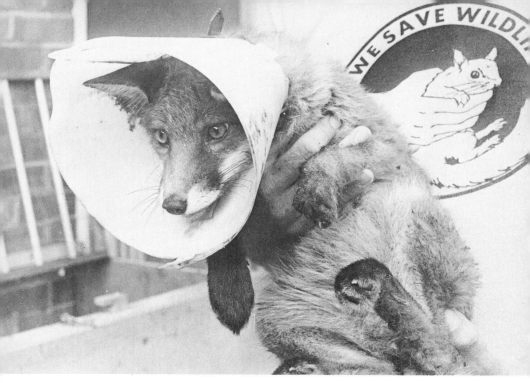

Traces of bright red new fur could be seen.

looked up and hated us each time we went to her box. Sometimes a permanently crippled animal has to be kept in captivity but it was obvious that Vix would never succumb to domesticity. She just had to get better and return to her wild existence.

After a week, the plaster and dressings had to be removed and the wounds checked for problems. Back at the surgery again Richard, expecting the worst, started to cut off the plaster with a pair of bone cutters. Every crunch of the cutters through the plaster seemed to shudder through the frail little body; although the wounds were healing, the bone damage on her toes would still have been very painful. Many of the nurses had got to know Vix and gathered round to see the outcome. I think we were all surprised but Richard was really jubilant – not only had the leg further improved but traces of bright red new fur could be seen where the skin had reformed. Her toes were also re-growing well, even fresh pads were forming.

However, the tendons were still somewhat contracted, meaning that once more Vix had to suffer the plaster and collar.

Another five weeks of confinement and plaster passed before, at last, she was able to flex her leg quite normally. We could discard the plaster and that collar and let her take over the cleaning of her leg. The only drawback now was the problem of handling her: with the collar on she had been easily handled as she could not turn and snap, now we had once again to resort to the grasper and gripping her by the scruff of her neck.

Foxes in the wild rely on their front legs for digging either to enlarge an earth or to cache away uneaten food. Vix had to be fully capable before we released her, so physiotherapy was the next stage we had to arrange. We prepared a pen for her; not very big, only 8 feet by 6 feet but with an earth floor and a small dark hutch where, for the first time since her captivity, she could hide away from the prying eyes of her captors.

From that moment on we saw very little of Vix; every morning her food had been eaten and her water bowl thrown in a corner. She started digging and, every night, fresh scrapes appeared in the hard soil and old pieces of meat were hidden away, all signs that her front leg had nearly regained its full strength. Every few days I had to extricate her from her den to see if she was healthy and that no fresh infection had flared up. She was not a very big fox but each time she fought me, so I had to be very confident in handling her otherwise she would have taken great delight in biting me. Her injured leg continued to improve, new pads formed until at last she was ready for release.

Somehow you sense when a patient is ready for release: birds show an urgency to fly even faster at their wire enclosures; kestrels especially start calling, harsh alarm calls that shatter the silence at any unusual movement. Vix's once random digging now seemed more concentrated, and a deep hole was forming in one corner of the pen. We decided to let her escape. The area of the hospital is free from hunting and shooting and many foxes have made their homes in the steep embankment of the nearby railway line. Once she had left, we could leave food out for her in case she had difficulty resettling in the wild.

47

We Save Wildlife

Then late one night a clamour of bird alarm calls from the aviaries told me that she was out. I saw her disappearing over the back fence. Much as we would have liked to protect her, the method of the Wildlife Hospital is to treat wild animals and birds then to let them return to the wild, so we had to leave her on her own.

However next morning when I went to clean her pen out, there were those defiant eyes glaring at me from the darkness of her den. She had obviously not settled on her first night out and had come back to safety at first light. In spite of all our fights she must have realized we were friends after all.

That night she went out again, and that was the last we saw of her. I could not help feeling for Vix and all she had been through. I hope she is doing well; my heart sinks every time we are called out to a fox casualty on this side of Aylesbury. It has never been her and it's now over a year since she left.

4

Now She Even Jumps

Most female deer, of any species, will leave their suckling youngsters hidden in deep grass while they go off to browse nearby. Fallow deer are no exception and, as they give birth during the two middle weeks of June, in early summer there are dozens of fawns lying alone in deep grass without any signs of caring parents. The casual walker may well stumble across one of these apparent orphans but a fawn should never be touched as human scent may well make a mother desert her offspring and as fallow deer fawns can be suckling well into October the waif is then condemned to a slow death by starvation. If you find a fawn it is imperative that you leave the area immediately or the mother may panic and still desert her offspring.

In spite of repeated warnings each year, we are still presented with 'orphaned deer' picked up by ill-informed well-wishers. It was late in July 1983 when we received a phone enquiry on how to look after a deer orphan. We guessed that this was another foolish fawn rescue and, knowing the difficulties of hand-raising deer, we suggested that the animal was brought to the hospital without delay; at least then it would have experienced care and the company of other young animals; since it must be a daunting experience for a young deer to be lifted from its world of grass and trees into the starkness of a house and the visitors who want to peer at the new arrival. At the hospital we respect an animal's timidity and try not to let it suffer too much exposure. In the wild if another animal stares at you, it intends to attack, so you imagine how a young deer feels with eyes threatening it every moment of the day.

The callers ignored all our warnings and declined to bring the fawn to us; we had a suspicion that they wanted to keep it as a pet, but they then informed us that the deer could not stand and asked if we could recommend any treatment that might help. As deer can stand almost from birth, there was obviously something drastically wrong but it is impossible to diagnose a problem on the telephone; there was no alternative, we told them, they must get the deer seen by a veterinary surgeon without delay.

The callers refused to give us their name, address or any clue to their whereabouts. We felt furious that yet another wild animal was being forced into domesticity, and frustrated that we could do nothing about it. Young deer are the most delightful of all the British mammals, and over the next few weeks it was very hard not to think of that frightened fawn without its mother and, for some reason, unable to stand.

Then, three weeks after the first telephone call, we received another from the same source. This time the news was even worse: not only had they not called in a vet but now the poor animal could not even lift its head. At times like this it is very difficult to stay calm but we knew that the only way to help this fawn was to talk to these people and make them see sense. Stressing the point that the deer was obviously dying had the desired effect and at last they gave us an address where the deer could be seen. Throwing a couple of blankets in the car I made one of my law-breaking dashes the fifteen miles to Gaddesden.

It was a large, old house with plenty of garden, and I wondered if they had intended to tame themselves a deer. As we went around the back of the property the sight that greeted us made tears well up in my eyes. I have never seen a sadder sight. The poor little fallow deer fawn lay spreadeagled on a patch of worn grass surrounded by boards about twelve inches high. She could not move, let alone escape, from her prison and the grass she was living on was dry enough for tinder with nowhere near enough nourishment for a growing animal. I was too choked – or was it angry – to say anything to the people; I just barged past them, wrapped the fawn in blankets and bundled her into the back of the car. Not only was she just skin, bone and light as a feather but, even worse, the flank on which she had been lying was one mass of weeping sores, pressure sores, which indicated that she had never even been turned over in all the weeks she had been there.

I laid Bambi on a warm fresh bed of barley straw.

Sue crouched in the back of the car to support the fawn's head and to try to comfort it for the journey back to Aylesbury. It just lay there looking at Sue with its enormous haunted deep-brown eyes. I stood on that accelerator but the car still would not go fast enough; I kept hoping that we could do something and were not too late.

The journey seemed to take forever. When we got home, I carried the helpless Bambi through to the hospital while Sue made an emergency call to one of the vets. Richard Hill answered the call, and Sue said he was practically in his car before he had put the phone down. While waiting, we mixed Bambi a warm drink of lamb's milk substitute, as cow's milk is quite unsuitable for deer and could quite easily have killed her. I had laid her on a warm, fresh bed of barley straw, where she looked as comfortable as possible but still flatly refused to sample the bottle of warm milk. In the wild she would still have been suckling from her mother, but perhaps her enforced

51

captivity had made her grow up too soon. Perhaps a bowl of milk was the answer? Sue transferred the warm milk to a bowl, then supported Bambi's head while I offered the food; no response whatsoever, so I gently pressed her nose into it. She licked the excess off her nose, liked it and proceeded to guzzle the bowl nearly dry. Just then Richard arrived. I think he was even more shocked on seeing her than we were at Gaddesden. I know his immediate thought was that Bambi had broken her back, as she had the classic symptoms: her legs were paralysed and she was only able to lift her head very slightly.

She would have to suffer a few tests so that Richard could try and trace the cause of her disabilities. He first pricked each of her legs with a needle; she moved at each contact, a sure sign that her central nervous system was intact. That meant there was hope: a broken spinal cord would have meant that there was no hope of recovery, but we could now show some optimism although Richard insisted that we should wait and see. Many other tests ensued until finally Richard diagnosed a massive vitamin E deficiency with complete atrophy of the muscles due to weeks of enforced recumbency. Many calves suffer with vitamin E problems, and usually one injection is sufficient to get them back on their feet, so after administering one dose to Bambi we could hope for some improvement by the following morning.

After the injection Richard turned his attention to the pressure sores. He had to roughly clean away any dead or infected tissue, there was no gentle way of doing it. I am sure that we all winced as much as Bambi but underneath all that rubbish most of the sores were only surface-deep; only the one on her inflamed hock looked to be severely infected. The sores would need to be cleaned twice daily with Dermisol Multicleanse Solution that would clear any dead tissue and would encourage regeneration and healing. The deep sore on her hock would need a course of antibiotic injections and the swelling would benefit from a course of cortisone. Richard's technique of tapping her rump before injecting had the desired effect of disguising the injection, she did not even flinch as the first antibiotics were administered.

Offering Bambi bowls of warm milk.

That night we laid her on her undamaged side, covered her with a blanket and settled her down with another bowl of warm lamb's milk. We had to bolster her up so that she rested on her keel and did not fall sideways and impede her digestive system. In the morning we hoped to see her standing, but she was lying in exactly the same position as when he left her. Richard, however, was not dismayed, he came out and gave her another booster of vitamin E. We could only wait, and during that day we pampered her, offering her bowls of warm milk and all the sorts of tit-bits so popular with deer: chickweed, chopped apples, rose petals and dandelion leaves which turned out to be her favourite nibble. I know deer are ruminants and eat enormous amounts of food but I was surprised how carefully Bambi chewed each mouthful before even thinking of another.

After another night, warm under the blanket, she still could not quite stand but at least she was now holding her head quite strongly

53

and there was some movement in those pitifully thin legs. Richard came out again but decided that her vitamin E quota was sufficient and that her inability to stand was now due only to the weakness in her muscles. The only course forward was to give her regular exercise and constant physiotherapy but the problem was how to exercise an animal that could not stand up. I could carry her; by supporting her body weight her legs would be free from any strain, but I could not possibly carry her for any length of time – she needed a hammock. But how do you suspend one to hold a deer? And how do you stop that deer from falling out? We have a wooden patio table with four legs about two feet long, and I thought that if I were to turn this upside down and screw two parallel bars across each pair of legs I could, possibly, then fix a blanket along these to support her stomach and chest, leaving her legs just clear of the base. With a few minor adjustments to suit her size, it worked perfectly and she hung there, gangly but off the ground for the first time in weeks. A small table set in front of her enabled us to offer her feed and water without her having to stretch to the ground. She seemed to appreciate the set-up and seemed to feel better, judging by the number of times she knocked the feed and water bowls off the table. Eventually I had to thwart her mischievous game by glueing the bowls to the table, but not before the base of her 'cradle' was spattered with all manner of soggy deer food.

The cradle proved absolutely ideal: I could get at the pressure sores to clean them and could keep her other flank free of similar problems, but best of all I could start her physiotherapy, moving each leg up and down encouraging her to push against me. Slowly this would build up the muscles that were letting her down.

At first I would only allow her to spend a few hours each day in her cradle but as she grew stronger I helped her exercise for longer and longer until she could push strongly with her front legs and eventually started to show improvement in her back legs. Out of the cradle she started to try and stand but would fall heavily time and time again. I tried to help her but as soon as my back was turned she would struggle up again then fall crazily across the garden. It was frightening to see her, she could so easily have crashed into a wall or

She hung there, off the ground for the first time in weeks.

fallen onto the concrete path, which I eventually had to cover with a
deep layer of blankets. I would spend every spare moment with her,
holding her body, letting her take some weight on those spindly,
wobbly legs. Each time I felt her balanced I would let her take all her
own weight; she would stand there for a few precious seconds then
her legs would buckle and she was down again. She tried so hard to
stay up and as the days went by her perseverance started to pay off as

she could stand for longer and I could start working her forward, encouraging those legs to move. At first they just dragged but gradually she put one front leg forward, then the other, but her back legs were still hopeless; she would need a lot more physiotherapy in the cradle before they would be of any use.

Out of the cradle, she still kept striving to stand up; she could manage to raise herself on her front legs, but as she lifted her rump those back legs would let her down and she would career across the grass, collapsing in an undignified heap. Over and over she tried and tried; we could not leave her in case she really did get into difficulties. Four days I sat outside with her, until one memorable morning, three weeks after she had arrived, she stood there for just a few seconds before she was down again. We both knew we were winning, and she tried again as I stood close by in case she needed help. First for seconds, then for minutes she stood there, then took one tentative wobbling step, then two, and then an uncontrollable gallop across the garden into the customary heap. All that day she practised until by evening she was quite good at standing and could manage to half walk and half run in the direction that she intended. She was exhausted. I was exhausted too, but I think that we were both ecstatically happy with the day's progress. Putting her into her shed that night, covering her with a blanket, I could almost hear her telling her friend the black-headed gull that slept perched on her back, of her great step forward that day.

From that day forth there was no looking back, as Bambi grew from strength to strength. The regular Dermisol treatment had nearly cleared the pressure sores although the stubborn sore on her hock still gave me some cause for concern but an X-ray showed that the bones of the joint were not infected, and it was only a matter of time before it healed. I asked Richard to check her teeth as a sore lump was appearing in the side of her cheek. It seemed that one of her teeth had a sharp protuberance on one side. As this is quite common in horses, most vets have a fast-cutting rasp that quickly files away the nuisance. Unfortunately not many deer have their teeth treated consequently Bambi had to suffer this enormous horse rasp in her somewhat small mouth, but happily one pull of the rasp

Three weeks after she had arrived, Bambi stood there.

was sufficient to remove the problem.

I would have thought that after all those weeks of indignity at the hands of humans Bambi would turn against people, but as is often the case with animals she did the unexpected, following me everywhere, nuzzling into my back if I had the audacity to ignore her. She loved nothing better than to tug everybody's shoe-laces undone, sucking them into a soggy mess before starting on jackets, ladies' dresses and cardigans all of which received her own, very damp, seal of approval. The amazing thing was that although she sucked everything within reach she never showed any aggression or desire to bite.

By this time she had completely ruined any lawn we had, her

sharp little hooves turned it to mud in no time at all. She had neatly cropped every growing plant within reach and had obviously relished two trays of cactus plants given to us for a fund-raising stall. Good growing grass is probably the best natural source of vitamin E and would be beneficial to Bambi's weakened condition and as we had two other lawns at the front of the house I felt that it was worth jeopardizing them just to see her fully recovered. The only drawback was that with the open-plan street, there were no fences so I had to erect a temporary three-foot chain-link fence so that Bambi could be grazed on the fresh grass. I never let her out there unsupervised which was just as well for one day two passing dogs spotted her and started barking. Luckily they were on leashes and controllable, but not Bambi; without hesitation she soared effortlessly over the three-foot fence and hurtled off down the road with me sprinting after her optimistically calling her name. I have never run so urgently in all my life, but Bambi seemed to be enjoying it, she could now jump and run nearly as well as any deer. At last she stopped and I, completely out of breath, gratefully grabbed her around the middle and somehow carried her back to safety. She was now so heavy it was hard to remember that she had weighed only thirty pounds when she first came to the hospital; she certainly had improved since those early desperate days. Needless to say, the front lawn was then off-limits, and she had to make do with any grass I could grow at the back of the house together with supplements of a coarse goat mixture, apples and, of course, the added vitamins.

Winter came and went; she grew the most luxuriant winter coat, thick and greasy. Snow and rain did not appear to bother her although in really severe weather I always made sure that she was snugly locked in her shed. It became increasingly difficult to find her fresh grass, she was a lot fitter, and I had to contemplate releasing her or else finding her more spacious quarters. I object to needlessly keeping wild animals in captivity, but during all those months of nursing and carrying her she had become unavoidably imprinted on me and there are a great many dangers in the wild. Apart from the hazards of roads and motorways there is a disturbing rise in the numbers of deer poachers and cullers, and it would have actually been cruel just to let her go. She needed to be moved to a large safe area where she would be protected – but we were worried that she would be lonely without the constant company she enjoyed at the hospital.

We had other deer pass through the hospital: Twinkletoes the baby muntjac, for instance, who grew up in the garden with Bambi. She was quite fit to be released and soon left the hospital. I went out one night to rescue a concussed fallow buck but once again it was soon fit enough for release. Then we had a call about a very young fallow buck who had been found by a road at Gaddesden, where Bambi came from. My usual breakneck driving brought him to the hospital, where we found that he had a badly infected compound fracture of one of his back legs. There was no way of saving the leg and, as I had seen three-legged deer cope very well in a protected environment, I agreed that the vets could amputate the leg in order to save the buck's life.

This was another deer that could not be released back to the wild, and we felt that fate had played its part in finding company for Bambi. After his operation and recovery, Fate (as we called him) had to suffer Bambi's old cradle until he built up enough strength to cope with his disability. Somehow Bambi could sense that he was in intensive care and when we brought him out in the cradle she nuzzled him and licked him as if to say, 'Don't worry, I was in that cradle once. You will soon be out of it.' She liked him, what a relief. We could now seriously plan moving the pair of them without the fear of Bambi pining for company.

As Fate grew stronger he was able to walk on his three legs within days of his operation, whereas Bambi had taken weeks even to be able to stand. I think it was only then that we realized just how weak she had been and how near to failing completely. Now the pair of them looked fit and content, and we arranged for them to have a fenced area inside a farm well away from traffic and poaching hazards but how could we transport them? Although I could still lift and carry Fate, Bambi was now too heavy and strong to manage and would panic inside any vehicle. The only answer was to sedate the pair of them.

'Don't worry, I was in that cradle once.'

We had arranged a Land Rover so that two of us could travel in the back with the deer. One injection of sedative and Fate was easy to manage, but not Bambi; she had to have three injections, and even then as two of us lifted her in a blanket she was still resisting. During the short journey, Fate, of course, was well behaved but Bambi, in the enclosed space at the back of a Land Rover, took great delight in causing all manner of panic as she constantly tried to climb into the front seats. However, we eventually arrived at our destination without any serious mishap. The deer were put in a large loose box with a heat lamp to keep them warm as the sedatives wore off; Bambi now was fast asleep, her sedative was working a little too late.

Bambi and Fate now live a somewhat pampered life on the farm; Bambi loves the open fields and likes nothing better than to 'pronk', with all four hooves off the ground, until she is gasping for breath; while Fate looks on, quite content to walk around on his three legs enjoying the new grass.

5

Oil!

Sue called me in from my morning round of the outside aviaries: 'It's the Inspector of Taxes' office on the phone, they want to speak to you.' Uneasily I took the receiver, expecting the worst. A young lady sounding very distressed had even worse news than I expected. 'There is oil all over the canal, the swans and ducks are covered in it. Can you do something?' The full horror of the situation dawned on me, since our local tax office overlooks the Aylesbury Basin of the Grand Union Canal and the office staff had seen the birds' distress from their office windows.

We had plenty of experience in catching the town's swans and ducks tangled in fishing line so we could estimate how many birds were in the area and likely to be affected by the oil. Our swan-catching equipment is always at the ready; with this and a pile of hessian sacks hurriedly thrown into the car we drove the short distance into the town centre and the canal basin car park.

The scene was horrifying: the once picturesque water scene of narrow boats and waterside tranquillity was covered with a lumpy rainbow-coloured pulp. Each narrow boat had a black rim of grime and the blanked-off end of the canal was a heaving, stinking mess of plastic bottles and other rubbish all covered with a clinging layer of oil. The British Waterways Board team was there even before us, fighting a retreating battle trying to stem the spread of the oil. A boom thrown across the canal was effectively preventing any further oil seeping into the basin but the damage, we had feared, had already happened; where the basin widened into a lagoon of about 400 square yards the resident family of swans was marooned in a sea of clinging oil.

The adult pair and their two remaining cygnets were trying in vain to rid themselves of the mess. Nothing is so gleaming white as a full grown swan in speckless plumage, which made the plight of these two adults with their fronts and sides matted with the black sludge appear even worse. Their two cygnets, still in their first year of life, also had their new grey feathers stained by the oil. Yet, as proud as ever, all four birds were concentrating on their preening, trying to restore their once immaculate feathers, and quite unaware that to swallow this stomach-burning oil was tantamount to committing suicide.

We had to act quickly and decisively if we were to save them and to clean them. We knew one of the owners of a narrow boat, Vic Herman. He was used to handling water birds and luckily was on board when we called. Using his telephone, we called in a close friend of ours, Charlie Norris, the local RSPCA Inspector, who has joined us on many swan rescues in the past.

At the time we did not have a powered boat so the only way to catch the swans was to try to entice them towards the bank with pieces of bread. Even with our swan hooks extended to their limits we still could not reach them, since they were only interested in their preening. We clapped our hands and stamped our feet but still they ignored us, all the time swallowing more and more oil.

We had to get afloat. Vic suggested using a cumbersome old floating bridge that the narrow boat owners used to maintain their craft. It was like a huge punt and had no means of propulsion but, being the only thing available, we decided to give it a try. With me perched precariously on one side and Vic on the other we pulled the punt along using the moored narrow boats as levers. We covered open stretches of water by pushing off and floating to the next anchor point. In spite of its bulk, the punt had the desired effect of forcing the swans to head in the direction we wanted.

Gradually we edged them towards a corner of the lagoon where Charlie was ready to catch the unwary birds. Perhaps I should not have said unwary, for as soon as they realized that the approach of our Dreadnought would seal off their escape they took evasive action, raised their wings and literally ran over the water and out of our trap, settling once more in the centre of the lagoon.

Where the canal ended there was a narrow channel lined with

narrow boats; our floating bridge could seal this channel and completely trap the swans in a small area where they could be reached. The only problem was to herd them towards the cul-de-sac when there was an alternative exit from the lagoon onto the main canal. One of the narrow boat owners solved the problem by swinging his boat across the open canal effectively blocking any escape route.

Once again Vic and I manhandled Dreadnought towards the swans. They responded by swimming out of the lagoon but happily chose our proffered escape route. Once we were behind them in the narrow channel Vic pulled us along the moored boats on his side, I did the same on the other. The swans didn't have enough room to take off so inch by inch we pushed them into the dead-end. We were now in sight of the Inland Revenue office windows and had quite an audience encouraging us.

Charlie was lying in wait as we approached. The cob (male) saw him and took over the vanguard of the small flotilla. Mute swans are very brave in defending their families, and this cob was playing his part to the full. Charlie however had seen it all before and, undaunted, promptly hooked the cob and pulled him clear of the water. I should explain that a swan hook is similar to a shepherd's crook and serves the same purpose. As a swan approaches, the hook can be placed comfortably round its neck, allowing it to be pulled into the bank. As Charlie demonstrated on that morning, the swan's wings are then held to its body preventing it from flapping and possibly injuring its captor.

The cob was put unceremoniously into a hessian sack. A hole had been cut in the closed end so that its head and neck could poke through. Swans do not appear to have the ability to escape backwards so any attempt to get out of the sack only results in them getting further into the closed end. This cob struggled, honked and hissed but soon settled and was put to one side well away from the water's edge.

Normally male swans are larger than their mates but strangely this pen (female) was enormous. Seeing the plight of her mate she made a dash for freedom down my side of the punt. As she tried to get through I grabbed her. I tucked her wings in, clasped her to me and slid her into another sack. Like the swans, Charlie and I now had a liberal coating of oil and canal water, and there were still two to catch.

Charlie lunged with his hook and secured one of the cygnets while I clambered over a narrow boat to capture the other. Unlike their parents the cygnets squeaked in distress, reminiscent of most young animals. However once all four birds were settled in the back of the car the distress calls changed to gurgles of welcome to each other.

There were no other swans on the canal but somewhere there were three Aylesbury ducks, the last survivors of a once world-famous cottage industry. Nets and hooks at the ready, we set off to quarter the canal. As we hurried along the towpath we could see the extent of the oil pollution. A drain near one of the factories was spewing more oil so that now the whole stretch of canal from the basin to the first lock was covered in a film of it. Luckily the lock prevented its spread up the canal to other wildlife sites. A narrow boat was ready to use the lock. This would have released the contamination but happily the owner saw our point and stayed clear.

The Aylesbury ducks are great favourites with the townspeople and usually congregate around a small baker's where they can solicit crumbs and titbits. True to form, there they were; three very bedraggled ducks. Like the swans their immaculate white feathers were now covered in clinging black oil.

We dragged the punt into position to ensure that the ducks could not get onto the water. Most species of duck can take off vertically to evade capture but Aylesbury ducks are too heavy to fly so we stood a chance. Using swan nets (somewhat like giant versions of the fishing nets we used as children to catch tiddlers) Charlie and I approached from either side. We caught one each but the remaining duck headed for the punt; quacking loudly she saw Vic ready to meet her. She turned and ran back towards me. I had passed my captured duck to Charlie so I made a desperate lunge as she passed and luckily caught her at my first attempt. We now had all three safely in cat boxes ready to go back to the hospital.

A last patrol of the canal side yielded no other birds, though we wondered about the plight of the water voles living in the banks. There was no way in which we could catch them, but we hoped that the Waterways Board would clear the canal before too much damage had been done.

The birds were very shocked at their ignominious capture, and we would not be able to attempt their cleaning for two or three days. To do so now would increase their stress and could result in heart failure. For the time being they were all put into the warmed garage to recover their composure. Feed and water would help ease their stress and clear some of the oil from their stomachs.

Although the damage to the feathers of an oiled bird is important our principal concern was the oil that had been ingested by our seven casualties. All birds take meticulous care of their plumage. Constant preening is the only way in which a bird, especially a water bird, can maintain the waterproofing and heat-retaining properties of their feathers. In their futile efforts to clean their feathers these birds must have swallowed quite a lot of oil. As most ingested oils cause severe inflammation of the birds' intestines, eventually leading to haemorrhagic enteritis and nephritis (inflammation of the kidneys), it was crucial that we treated these casualties before the internal damage was too severe.

Over the years many groups have seen rescued birds die even before any oil was cleaned from their feathers. Recently a kaolin-based tablet used for stomach disorders in dogs and cats has proved effective in treating oil-induced intestinal disorders in birds. Although we are at Britain's farthest point from the coast and do not receive many oil victims, I always carry in stock a large bottle of Kaobiotic tablets just in case.

We had to dose the seven birds twice daily until their droppings showed no further traces of oil. To make sure that each bird received its prescription I had to literally kneel with each swan between my knees and hold firmly onto its head and neck. Sue then forced open each beak and put the tablets as far down their throats as possible. As you release your swan it jumps up, flaps its wings, regains its dignity and swallows the tablet. It may sound simple, but after all seven birds had been dosed, the garage was a mess of oil, feathers and water. We had to do this twice every day.

We then left the birds with ample supplies of corn and bread in water. Feeding would help to flush the oil from their intestines but we had to make sure that the water bowls were small otherwise all seven birds would have happily bathed, which would have prompted them to preen thereby ingesting yet more oil.

We were all exhausted by this time and decided to leave the birds to settle down and for us to recover. A fresh appraisal of their condition could be made the following morning.

We had noted that both adult swans had rings on their legs. These were British Trust for Ornithology rings put on under their licence when the birds were younger. The BTO could tell us something of the birds' history and add to the national records of swan movements. The male swan's ring was numbered Z 20691. Reference to the BTO computer showed him to be amazingly over 18 years old, one of the longest surviving wild swans on record. He originated near Reading, so presumably had left the lead-polluted Thames at an early age to flourish on the cleaner backwaters of Buckinghamshire, over thirty miles away. His mate also had a history. She was over 11 years old but had been ringed locally in Wendover.

Over the next three days their voluminous diet and twice-daily Kaobiotic tablets helped them clear their systems of all traces of oil. Their droppings, which were initially full of oil, were now clear of contaminant so we could contemplate setting up the washing process.

Sadly one of the cygnets got steadily weaker. It was eating with the other birds but seemed to be losing weight and energy. Its droppings, although clear of oil, showed ominous traces of blood; the oil had taken its toll. Usually we isolate any bird that is sick but we did not want to subject this cygnet to added stress by taking it away from the family unit. We continued his treatment after the others had ceased theirs. In spite of everything he grew weaker and weaker. I am sure that the closeness of this little family gave him comfort as he slowly faded. Then one evening he could not stand on his own. We wrapped him in a blanket in front of the heater in the hope that he might pick up. By the morning he had died. Though we could not save him, at least he was warm and with his family when he died, not cold and alone on some freezing canal bank. We had never lost a swan before.

A post mortem carried out by our vets showed that the oil had killed him. His internal organs were black with the contamination; he had obviously preened too vigorously during those first few hours of the spillage.

As the actual washing process is a physically traumatic experience for oiled birds we had given our six remaining casualties four days to settle and to get used to being handled. They looked fine and strong; we then had the daunting task of trying to restore their shattered plumage.

The University of Newcastle upon Tyne has carried out lengthy research into the washing of oiled birds. Their findings and recommendations have now been adopted by most bird cleaning centres. They found that using a 2% solution of Co-op washing-up liquid at 45 Centigrade produced the most effective cleaning. The birds are immersed in the solution for ten seconds. Then, while one person holds the bird, another works the solution up and into its plumage separating each feather to make sure that every trace of oil is lifted. Once the oil is loose the bird then has to be rinsed in running hot water again at 45.

To wash three swans and three Aylesbury ducks would require gallons of Co-op washing-up liquid and literally hundreds of gallons of running hot water. There was no way in which we could cope in the small hospital area, we had to find an alternative site to carry out the washing.

The Co-operative Wholesale Society kindly sent us down enough washing-up liquid and I had the bright idea of asking the local council if we could commandeer their vehicle depot. The depot has running hot water for cleaning the council's lorries but more importantly it also has an efficient filtered drainage system to dispose of all that contaminated water. We have always found Aylesbury Vale District Council to be very helpful, and on this occasion they willingly offered the facilities for the following Saturday morning.

I could foresee only one other problem: how do you immerse a

I immersed the female swan for about ten seconds.

fully grown swan in hot soapy water? What do you put the water in? What we needed were some of those old tin baths that were once so common. However, hardware dealers no longer stock or sell tin baths. Sue made a few phone calls to some of our volunteer helpers. Before long we had two tin baths; although one did leak slightly it was not enough to hinder the washing operations.

On the following Saturday morning we packed the swans in their sacks and the ducks in boxes and made for the depot. Some of our volunteer helpers had asked to be included on any work with oiled birds. These birds would be ideal for training the volunteers as they were unlikely to encounter any oiled bird larger than a swan. A few of the council's workers had stayed at the depot to show us how to work the pressure cleaning machine.

I measured out the required amount of washing-up liquid to mix a 2% solution in one of the tin baths. The thermometer I had brought

Oil!

to measure the required 45 was glass, my first mistake. With soapy hands I picked it up to test the first tub but it shot out of my hands and shattered on the floor. I knew 45 was approximately as hot as a human hand could stand comfortably so undaunted I added hot water using my hand as the thermometer.

Charlie and I had the experience of handling many swans so we decided to wash the first bird, the large female. Charlie supported her weight while I immersed her for about ten seconds. With Charlie continuing to hold her, I then worked the hot water into each of her feathers. It was tiring work and I could see Charlie straining to take her weight. The washing had to be carried out methodically until every trace of oil was lifted. I extended her immense wings and 'unzipped' each of her flight feathers in order to give them individual attention. She flapped and grunted, there were suds, oil and soapy water everywhere yet it was amazing how that 2% solution lifted the oil from her plumage. The water became blacker as she started to look white again.

There were suds, oil and soapy water everywhere.

We Save Wildlife

After about 15 minutes I decided that she was clean enough so I started the hot water hose ready to rinse her off. Every trace of oil and washing-up liquid had to be rinsed from her feathers, any trace left behind would allow water and cold to seep in and destroy her waterproofing. The machine was now pumping out hot water at about the right temperature. I jetted it under and into each feather, starting on her back, then her sides and wings and finally onto her underneath. Swans have a very dense layer of down under the top feathers, and these needed extra attention as it trapped much of the washing solution.

A bird's plumage is surely one of the marvels of the natural world; as the water was hosed into the bird's feathers they became increasingly dry until when all the oil and washing-up liquid had been

Every trace of oil and washing-up liquid had to be rinsed off.

rinsed out the water ceased to dampen the feathers but simply formed beads and ran off. To the amazement of the trainee helpers this swan gradually became dry until after about twenty minutes she was gleaming white once again. We had equipped the back of one of the estate cars with a fan heater to keep the washed birds warm while the others were cleaned. The female swan was settled in and soon started to preen her dishevelled feathers back into place.

Now it was time to show our helpers how to wash the rest of the birds. The cleaning went without a hitch and a few hours later all the birds were secure in the heated car. In spite of our waterproofs we were all soaked through and ready for hot drinks back at the hospital.

The birds were kept in the garage overnight with a fan heater preventing any of them getting chilled. After a few days in an outside pen they could all be released. As Aylesbury ducks are not truly wild birds we had to find them a new home. This was not difficult as over the years we have built up a network of suitable sites not just for the release of wild creatures but also for the resettlement of displaced domestic birds.

On the following Tuesday we took the ducks to their new home. They were soon swimming in their own pond quacking in unison, and seeming to celebrate their new found freedom. The whole town of Aylesbury had followed the progress of the swans with local newspaper staff accompanying us on the release the following day. All our swan releases are onto the huge Wilstone reservoir near Tring. We have found it large enough to accommodate more than one family of swans and as it is not popular with anglers there is the minimum of danger from lead and discarded tackle.

It was pouring with rain as we set out for Wilstone. A reporter and photographer from the *Bucks Herald* followed in a separate car. We had warned them that Wilstone can be very muddy but I still do not think they were ready for the quagmire that greeted us. Sue and I were used to this type of weather and made sure we were well insulated against the cold and wet. We carried the swans, in their sacks, the last hundred yards to the water's edge. The male went first, revelling in the fresh water, but still waiting for his mate and

We carried the swans the last hundred yards.

cygnet to follow him. All three sailed off across the water, every now and then ducking under and shaking their feathers back into place.

A happy ending, or so we thought. The following evening the telephone rang; it was Vic. 'Your swans are back on the canal.' We asked him to keep the swans in the cleaned stretch of water until we could get there. This time we would borrow a rowing boat which one of our helpers could bring over from Tring.

It was cold, dark and wet when we arrived at the canal, the sort of night when it's better not to leave the fireside. Vic had kept the swans at bay away from the last remaining oil but we could not leave them there. Birds are simple-minded creatures that invariably find a hazard if there is one. With the death of the cygnet still on our minds we knew that we could not take the chance of them getting back into that oil.

A stalwart helper volunteered to take the first stint of rowing the boat; he stepped in, sorted his oars and started for the swans. In the light of our torches we could see he was going around in circles. I called to him, 'Have you ever been in a boat before'? 'No,' he replied. 'I bet you can't even swim.' Once again, 'No.' He still insisted on rowing and as the water is comparatively shallow I had no option but to let him carry on. Thankfully, after a few more minutes of aimless spinning, he mastered a rowing technique and set off after the swans.

This time he managed to drive the swans into a small offshoot of the canal. They were trapped so it was reasonably easy for me to climb the guard fence and capture each one.

Once again we took them to Wilstone but this time I clipped the ends off the flight feathers on their wings. This would effectively prevent them flying back to the canal at least until they had moulted a new set of feathers, by which time the canal would be completely free of oil.

6

Godzilla

Every year we look forward to the month of November: all our intake of young birds and animals have grown and been released; the animals of the countryside can find plenty of food without venturing onto the hazard of the highway; the summer visitors, the swallows, martins and warblers have left for warmer climes and our winter influx of redwings and fieldfares has not yet started. We have fewer casualties in November than in any other month, the temporary lull gives us a chance to catch up on the jobs we had to ignore in the fever of the summer months. November 1983 was very typical; little was happening, few casualties were found needing our help. We were taking stock, analysing the record cards of the nearly two thousand patients we had cared for that year, when a call came in to break the monotony of all that office work: a heron had been found crouched in a field as a local farmer sprayed his crops. Thinking it strange that the bird did not fly at his approach, the farmer had collected it up and was bringing it to the hospital.

Herons are always challenging patients but the thought of this one being dowsed in herbicide filled me with dreadful memories of the one and only merlin ever brought to the hospital. The merlin is one of our rarest birds of prey and is in danger of extinction. This bird smelt of diesel oil and insecticide; it too had been sprayed by a farmer, and horrifyingly died within hours of its arrival at the hospital. There was nothing we could do, and I hoped that the heron was not about to suffer a similar fate.

The casualty arrived wrapped in an old trench coat: I was ready for the yellow dagger beak that herons aim so accurately at any unprotected eye, but as I uncovered the bird's head a much shorter blackish beak shot out, grazing my wrist as I hastily withdrew. This was not a heron, but I must admit that I was not sure what type of

74

A large bird with a glistening black back, each feather tipped with a thin scallop of grey.

bird it was. I gingerly unwrapped the rest of the bird, while maintaining a firm grip on that beak, and discovered a large bird with a glistening black back and each feather tipped with a thin scallop of grey. The chest and underneath feathers gleamed white, typical of all swimming birds as it breaks up their silhouettes as they hunt on the surface of the water above their fish prey. The short legs with large webbed feet situated at the back end of the bird suggested a diver but he was quite unlike the strikingly handsome colourful birds I had seen in all the bird books. He seemed quite unmoved by his experiences and, judging by his hostile nature and lack of that diesel smell, I assumed most of the herbicide spray had missed him.

He was very large, well over two feet long, far too big to fit in one of our normal heated hospital cages. I keep a child's play pen for larger casualties and soon settled Godzilla on a fresh dry base of paper towels. Godzilla seemed, at the time, to be a very appropriate name;

every time I went near him or picked him up he would lunge at me, sometimes successfully but thankfully more often than not I managed to avoid his intentions. Having his legs situated so far back on his body helped him swim superbly, but on dry land, or in a play pen, he was quite unable to stand or move around and consequently was far more manageable.

I could find no records of a diver being kept in captivity so had to improvise, trying to emulate his natural diet and conditions. I normally have a small stock of frozen sprats for herons and other larger fish-eating birds and animals, and Godzilla soon learnt that the inert fish in the stainless steel bowl were as good as anything freshly caught off the Scottish coast from where he probably originated. Having had experience of other birds living entirely on white fish I knew there was a danger that the enzyme thiaminase contained in these fish could eventually break down Godzilla's natural thiamine (vitamin B1), causing nerve damage and certain death. I had found a tablet designed primarily for fish-eating captive dolphins and killer whales. These contained extra vitamin B1 and if fed daily to Godzilla would ensure that no deficiencies occurred. Mind you, holding him, forcing open his beak and putting the large tablet deep into his throat was not something I was looking forward to but with Sue's help the first pill was pushed into his throat and swallowed without too much damage to any of us.

We assumed that he came from Scotland as the occasional ringed diver had been seen around the south coast in winter but he may well have flown in from one of the Scandinavian countries; he caused quite a stir among the local birders, some of whom had never seen a diver and certainly never at such close quarters. Nobody, not even the experts, could decide which species of diver we were caring for. Apparently both the red-throated and the black-throated diver have remarkably similar winter plumage. The trust's scientific adviser, Dr Philip Burton, had experience of illustrating the various facets of a diver's plumage and it was he who finally identified Godzilla as a black-throated diver, *Gavia arctica*. The most striking difference between the two species is the slightly upward curve of the red-throated's bill compared with the straight dagger of the black-throated. Both species breed in Scotland but the black-throated seems to prefer the remote tarns of the extreme north.

Thankfully Godzilla was not one of those nervous birds that hide themselves and sometimes do not bother to feed; he had obviously had very little contact with humans and readily displayed an interest in any visitor, interspersing each visit by picking up and swallowing every sprat I could set before him. He ate so many fish that my stock of sprats diminished rapidly. Fishmongers sometimes carry sprats but very rarely had the number I required. There was a simple way around the problem, which was to make an early morning visit to Billingsgate Fish Market, now in the heart of London's dockland. The following day, well before dawn, Sue and I set off down the M1 to London. Arriving early, we were amazed that most of the day's transactions seemed to have been already completed. We wandered around the main hall trying to decide who did and who did not have sprats. Eventually we broached the subject with one of the dealers and he pointed out where we were likely to find sprats and, even more importantly, another dealer who stocked sand eels, the diet of many of Britain's coastal fishing birds. We bought two cases of sprats and a case of sand eels and set off back to Aylesbury before the London rush hour hemmed us in.

The defrosted sprats and sand eels gave Godzilla the best of breakfasts. After this and his vitamin pill I decided to try him on water but as we are somewhat limited for space his artificial loch would have to be the family bath. As he was used to the icy waters around the north of Scotland we had to make the bath as cold as possible and ran the cold water tap until the temperature dropped so much that it was uncomfortable even to put my arm in. Godzilla loved it. He changed from the helpless bird we had known in the play pen into a streamlined torpedo. Those enormous feet, so useless on land, now propelled him up and down the bath at terrifying speed. He revelled in his natural element. One second he was speeding along under water, the next he was literally standing on the water splashing the spray into every corner of the bathroom. Dropping a few sprats into the water brought out the hunter in him; one by one they were torpedoed, turned on end and swallowed head first.

Godzilla's feathers had absorbed some water.

I did notice that his feathers had absorbed some water; possibly his encounter with the farmer's spray had temporarily upset his water repellency. As wet plumage can be very damaging to birds I could not afford to let him get chilled so I resorted to drying him off in the airing cupboard where he was soon steaming and vigorously preening his feathers back into condition. So far so good.

In order to overcome this temporary loss of water-repellency Godzilla would have to bathe regularly, as only his preening could rectify the situation. Not being able to stand on dry land, he could only preen his under-feathers when he was splashing up and down in the bath but after a few days I found that he could spend longer in the water before showing any signs of getting wet.

Assuming that he would soon be completely fit, we would then have to decide when and where to release him. There were no other black-throated divers within hundreds of miles of Aylesbury and we had no guarantee, if he were to be released locally, that he could fly back to Scotland. He had to be set free off the west coast of Scotland where he could live quite naturally and possibly find a mate in the following spring. We could carry him north by car but although our faithful Ford Escort does sterling service around the Home Counties it would probably never recover from a journey of over five hundred miles. An appeal was put out by BBC television for a suitable method of transporting Godzilla to Scotland. We had all manner of offers from open-topped sports cars to Rolls Royces, but the most suitable had to be that of British Airways who offered to fly me and Godzilla from Heathrow to one of the larger Scottish airports. We accepted their offer most gratefully and although I had a phobia about flying and had never flown before I knew that flying Godzilla to Scotland was the surest way of protecting him from the stress of a long car journey. I had been the only person to handle Godzilla during his confinement so there was no alternative, I had to go.

Preparing Godzilla for release involved having him ringed in order to monitor his survival or demise in the wild. Philip Burton, who is one of our ringers, was in a quandary when he came to ring Godzilla: the manual of bird ring sizes does not recommend a size for black-throated divers. Apparently so few have ever been ringed that the size was left entirely to the ringer's discretion. To add to this difficulty, a diver's legs are flattened front to back – presumably to lessen any drag as they are swimming – so any ring had to be moulded elliptically in order that it could move freely up and down the leg, but would not slide over or impede the foot and ankle joints.

We Save Wildlife

As always, I held the bird while Philip fitted the ring and somehow I suffered from Godzilla's stabbings whereas Philip remained unscathed.

Godzilla, with the new 'bangle' on his leg, continued to feed well. His 'killer whale' tablets had kept any thiamine deficiency at bay and now he could spend any amount of time in the bath without showing signs of dampness. He was ready to go.

Joyce Monk at British Airways was making all the arrangements for the flight. She told me that Concorde was flying to Scotland later that week and asked, would I like to take Godzilla supersonically thus cutting down the travelling time to a minimum? How could I refuse to make my maiden flight in Concorde; I was almost beginning to look forward to the trip.

BBC Television had followed the story of Godzilla and wanted to film the whole journey until his eventual release. As we rely heavily on public support to run the hospital we always welcome any media coverage. A success story of this nature would certainly boost our project to be able to care for more and more wildlife casualties.

Everything was prepared; Concorde was ready to fly on Friday, BBC Television together with many local and national newspapers had booked their seats, Godzilla was ringed and full of fish and even I was packed although they would not let me take a parachute with me.

Then on the Tuesday morning when I went in to take Godzilla for his morning bath, there was no welcoming lunge, nothing; Godzilla was lying flat and still on the bottom of the playpen. I could not believe it; everything had been going well, he had always eaten and bathed exuberantly, he had shown no symptoms of being ill. What could have happened?

Sue somehow managed to phone all those people who had shown such concern over Godzilla's welfare. I had to find out why he died. The country's finest wildlife laboratories are at the Monks Wood Experimental Station in Huntingdon; I knew that Mike French there had considerable experience in autopsies on swans that had died from lead and other poisons. He kindly agreed to carry out a post mortem if I could get Godzilla to him without any delay.

Provided they are sealed in two polythene bags, biological specimens can be sent by first class post, so, neatly cocooned in the requisite packaging, poor Godzilla got his journey north but not in the manner we wanted.

Mike French received the body the following morning and carried out an immediate post mortem. On opening the bird's chest cavity he instantly found a choking mass of the fungus aspergillus. Godzilla had died of the disease most dreaded by all who care for sick birds, aspergillosis. The disease often shows no symptoms and cannot be diagnosed in the living animal. Nor is there any cure for it. It appeared that Godzilla had the disease even before he was found by the farmer, and exposure to the contaminated air of inland Britain had only exaggerated his condition.

I now believe any sea bird that arrives inland can be carrying the first traces of the fungus which will explode into growth while the bird is in the confined atmosphere of inland Britain. Since losing Godzilla I now use an anti-fungus gel manufactured for human use. So far no other of my seabird casualties has died of aspergillosis, so perhaps Godzilla did not die in vain.

7

Percy the Street Urchin

There are so many pigeons flying about London that you could easily imagine an injured or sickly bird going unnoticed in the hubbub of passing traffic. However, there are people concerned with the plight of individual birds and when these good Samaritans take the trouble to carry a casualty the forty miles to Aylesbury then you realize why we are renowned as a nation of animal lovers.

Percy was brought to us by such a good Samaritan, a lady who had gone to the trouble and expense of hiring a mini-cab just to bring him to the hospital. She had met the usual apathy experienced by Londoners in that nowhere could be found in the capital that would even consider treating 'a pigeon'. She had phoned us in desperation; I just hoped that we could do something for the poor bird.

On his arrival Percy was booked in by Sue, who filled out a record card that would give me details of the bird's dilemma. We find these record cards invaluable both as a source of reference and as a permanent record of all our casualties. Percy's record card simply stated 'Adult feral pigeon with multiple injuries probably the result of a road traffic accident.' It is my task to evaluate the extent of any injuries, if necessary arranging X-rays of damaged areas with no obvious lesions.

In the surgery I opened Percy's travelling box, and could see by his posture that he had at least some serious leg damage. Each leg was crooked at a totally unnatural angle, a sure sign of fractures or dislocations. His right wing was splayed to the side, and it too looked as if it was fractured. Without even temporary splints there was a danger that he might try to flap that broken wing. Birds have little sensation of pain so there was a distinct possibility that, on movement, the broken bone ends could pierce the skin, opening the injury to infection and in turn seriously jeopardizing any chance of healing. A bird may also try to walk on fractured legs with the same disastrous outcome. Strapping the damaged wing and both legs to Percy's body prevented any movement and kept him quiet until I had made preparations to investigate and securely splint each damaged bone.

My preparations involved having ready any instruments, splints or dressings that I might need. A Weetabix box and a pair of scissors are essential for cutting out cardboard wing splints. Knowing that both legs were fractured, I also had to arrange to keep Percy from trying to stand for at least three weeks, the time it takes for avian bones to form sufficient new growth to support any weight. My solution is a home-made cradle from which I can suspend a bird, keeping it clear of the base board. A simple square of plywood with a twelve-inch upright at each corner and two diagonal cross-pieces connecting the tops of those uprights proves sufficient for most perching birds.

Splinting and strapping the injured wing and then suspending him would allow me free access to work on splinting his legs. Since I did not want to cause any further damage to his legs I carefully laid him on layers of fresh towelling and covered his head (which quietens most birds and prevents unnecessary stress). He settled immediately so I was able to gingerly feel along his injured wing until I found the rough ends of the broken bone lying just below the skin. The broken bone was the ulna, the larger of the two bones connecting the elbow to the wrist, an identical arrangement to that of the human arm. As I have said, birds feel little or no sensation of pain so I was able to stretch the wing and re-align the ends of the broken ulna without Percy even flinching. The bone then had to be immobilized for the three weeks so I cut a simple splint out of my Weetabix packet and secured it with ultra-sticky zinc-oxide plaster. I find that zinc-oxide is the one plaster that birds cannot remove and can even resist the attention of strapped crows and rooks with their powerful beaks.

With the wing securely strapped I could then suspend Percy from

I passed two strips of zinc oxide under Percy's body.

the cradle by passing two more strips of zinc-oxide plaster diagonally under his body and then up and over the two cross-members. Making sure that the plaster crossed on his sternum prevented it impeding his swallowing and breathing ability.

With Percy suspended about four inches above the base of the cradle I could then see the extent of the damage to his legs. His left leg was fractured just above the ankle joint. Just like the fractured ulna in his wing, the fractured bone, the tibia, had overlapped and had to be pulled into line before a splint could be applied. The strength of a pigeon's leg muscles showed as their contraction made it necessary for me to exert quite a force in order to stretch the leg and bring the broken ends together. Once again Percy seemed oblivious to my manhandling his fractures – he seemed more interested in pecking at the plaster tapes keeping him suspended. With the fracture reduced and the bone held straight, I then fitted a padded

84

aluminium splint, once again held in place by plenty of zinc-oxide plaster. The padding on the splint allowed for any swelling of the soft tissues around the injury without restricting any blood supply.

With the leg now fixed in a more natural position, I noticed that poor Percy's toes were hanging limply without any apparent support. Gently manipulating them confirmed that all three forward toes were also fractured. Cutting a four-pointed star out of my Weetabix packet I strapped it flat under his foot effectively holding the fractured toes where they ought to have been. The fourth point of the star was merely to support Percy's undamaged rear toe while he was in traction.

Turning the cradle round I could manipulate the other leg, and this time discovered that the metatarsus below the ankle joint was the damaged bone. A padded aluminium splint immobilized that while another cardboard star supported three more fractured toes.

Percy had accepted his predicament.

We Save Wildlife

After checking again that the supporting tapes were not obstructing his front or back ends I suspended food and water dishes just within reach of his beak. He obviously accepted his predicament for without further ado he dipped his head in the water dish and drank, unperturbed by my presence. Unlike most birds which have to lift their heads to swallow water, pigeons and doves have the ability to siphon water up through their beaks. Presumably this is a modification of their feeding habits when in the nest. The young pigeon will force its head into a parent's throat in order to siphon up the 'pigeon's-milk' which is its complete nourishment for the first weeks of life.

Thankfully Percy continued to be a model patient. I have seen birds suffer depression and give up the will to live but not Percy, he seemed resigned to being trussed up and fed normally throughout his confinement. His strappings stayed intact, all I had to do was top up his food and water and regularly change the newspaper covering the base of the cradle.

After two and a half weeks I cut away the plaster and splints on his legs and toes. His right leg still appeared weak so I re-splinted it just to be on the safe side. He could now move the other leg and flex his toes, which would help build up the muscles damaged in the accident and wasted by the weeks of inactivity. At this time I felt it unwise to unstrap the wing in case he flapped it and damaged it against the uprights of the cradle.

However four days later when I did cut away the strapping there were no signs of movement along the ulna, so there was every possibility that with practice he would soon be flying again.

Taking Percy down from the cradle resulted in dozens of feathers coming away as I pulled off the zinc-oxide straps. Pigeon feathers are very loosely mounted and can be pulled out without any effort. This is probably a very good escape tactic; you can imagine many predators being left with a mouthful of feathers while their prey has flown. I was not worried by Percy's new nakedness, he would soon grow a new set of feathers. I prefer to pluck the feathers rather than cut the tape off as a plucked feather will soon be replaced whereas a cut feather will not be replaced until the next annual moult, possibly months ahead. Within a few weeks Percy's now dishevelled plumage would be back to its former prime condition.

Percy had been in intensive care for three weeks, and to put him outside now could result in him catching a chill. A large cage in intensive care would serve for a few days until he had regained his balance and the remaining leg splint could be taken off. A bird's skeleton is so light that any strapping applied to a wing will unbalance it for a few hours until it has learnt to compensate for the added weight. Similarly the removal of Percy's strapping had the same effect and the first day in the new cage I regularly found him upside down with his legs waving in the air. Lining the bottom of the cage with old carpet helped him to get a grip with the claws of his good leg and by the second day he had mastered the problem, standing normally and even using the splinted leg to support himself.

Cutting away the remaining splints.

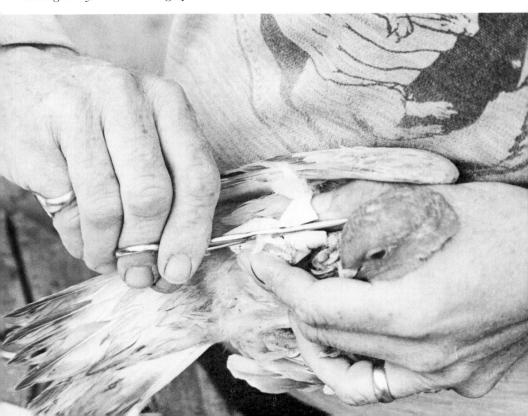

We Save Wildlife

His injured wing was still very stiff but he was able to move it slightly. I subjected him to regular bouts of physiotherapy, stretching the wing to its full extent and flexing the muscles until a few days later, when I removed the final leg splint, he could flap the wing almost as strongly as the other, although he did carry it slightly lower.

With both legs unhindered he was managing to walk, albeit a little deliberately. He was now fit enough to be introduced to the other pigeon patients in an outside aviary.

As I put him into the aviary many of the other pigeons flew down to investigate the new arrival. At first he was a trifle subdued but he soon spotted the large bathing bowl, took a long drink and then jumped in, splashing water everywhere as he soaked and preened every feather soiled by his weeks of confinement.

He soon proved to be a very dominant cock bird; strutting around, chest out, cooing his superiority. He now had the pick of roosting places and was always first at the freshly topped up grain dish. His flying had improved so much that after a month in the aviary we could consider releasing him. Although there are some feral pigeons flying about Aylesbury we felt that he stood a better chance of survival on the outskirts of London and as we were due to make a trip to Hampstead we decided to take him with us.

The day on which we drove down to London was ideal flying weather, no rain and just the merest whisper of a breeze; Percy travelled on the back seat in a dark pigeon carrying case. On the edge of Hampstead Heath we took him out of the box. A quick blink to get accustomed to the light and he was off, flying strongly to a tall horse chestnut tree. He looked superb, so, satisfied, we drove on to our appointment in the village never expecting to see Percy again. He had other ideas.

When we arrived back in Aylesbury later that day there was Percy sitting on top of the aviary voicing his return to the other pigeons. It was obvious that wherever I released him he would always expend every effort to get back to Aylesbury. I did not want to keep him in captivity so shooed him away but only as far as a neighbouring house. We have experienced this pigeon behaviour before, and

We found Percy sitting on top of the aviary.

eventually the birds will leave after finding themselves more hospitable accommodation.

Percy continued to come back for many months. He obviously had found somewhere to roost overnight but, knowing that grain was always available at the hospital, he always made us the first call on his daily itinerary. One day he turned up with a smaller pigeon by his side. Assuming she was a hen bird it seemed that Percy had made his mark on the local population. She was more shy than Percy, always hanging back until after he had flown in and settled into the grain dishes. Pigeons make very loyal partners, and Percy and his ladyfriend were inseparable. For many weeks they came for their early morning feast and then suddenly they came no more. We liked to believe that they had set up home somewhere but in the back of my mind there is always the thought that they may have fallen foul of a shotgun or air rifle. Whenever a pigeon flies in we look for Percy; perhaps one day he will show up.

89

We Save Wildlife

Some people say to me, 'Why bother with pigeons, there are so many of them?' I have a sobering reply to the question: the American Passenger Pigeon was once the most prolific bird on earth. It is now extinct!

8

Chestnut

Most young squirrels brought to the hospital are suffering from internal bleeding, the result of poisoning with warfarin. It appears to me that even suckling squirrels suffer the effects of their mothers having eaten poisoned grain. The antidote for warfarin is vitamin K, but once the internal haemorrhaging has started, it is too late to save an animal. When he was brought in during October 1982, Chestnut had no signs of warfarin poisoning, his gums showed pink and healthy especially in contrast to his bright orange incisor teeth. When an animal is bleeding internally the blood drains from its gums leaving them characteristically very pale and white; only blood transfusions can help but as yet there is very little experience in this branch of animal medicine.

Chestnut was a very young squirrel found in a wood at High Wycombe about 15 miles from the hospital. He had obvious wounds to his hindquarters which had paralysed his legs and tail, allowing his rescuers Mr and Mrs Parker to pick him up. Checking his gums showed no internal bleeding but I still handled him very gently in case he had taken some warfarin poison that could cause a blood vessel to burst. Knowing that squirrels' razor-sharp incisor teeth can inflict a nasty bite I wrapped his head in a small towel before inspecting the wounds on his back. The towel had the effect of calming his stress at being handled and also protecting me should he decide to bite.

One of his back legs had two holes in it similar to those caused by a dog bite. Slight pressure oozed pus from both wounds so it seemed that some days had elapsed since they were inflicted and a massive infection had set in. Antibiotics were needed without any delay. Penicillin would stem the infection but it had to be a precisely measured dose for several days only. Squirrels, being herbivorous, rely on natural gut bacteria to break down the cellulose contained in the majority of their food. Any excess of antibiotic could destroy this bacteria, causing serious digestive problems. Feeding on natural yoghurt could restore any destroyed bacteria but with an animal in Chestnut's condition it would be better if he did not have to cope with any unnecessary complications.

To set the penicillin working immediately I decided to inject Chestnut before we attempted to clean up his wounds. I weighed him so that I could calculate a precise dose, which I injected intramuscularly into the top of his undamaged back leg. He would have a further injection each day for the following six days.

While I was involved in this first injection Sue had made up an antiseptic solution of Savlon and hot water. She then held Chestnut's covered head as I set about cleaning out the wounds. Using a 20 millilitre syringe fitted with a long spout I jetted the Savlon into the wound. Irrigating any abscess in this way flushes out any putrid or foreign material leaving the wound clean and able to heal from the inside. As abscesses must heal from the inside I had to make sure that the wounds were kept open and did not seal any infection under the skin.

The way to a young animal's heart is with a warm bottle of Lactol so when the first aid was finished Sue settled down to feed Chestnut while I telephoned the vet to ask him to call in on his way home that evening. Chestnut must have been starving for he did not hesitate when offered a pipette full of warm Lactol, he reached up with both front paws, gripped the pipette and eagerly guzzled it empty. This habit of gripping the pipette is peculiar only to squirrels; it's very rewarding to see the obvious delight they find in feeding. Most young mammals will settle for 4 − 8 pipettes of Lactol, and when their mouths remain full they are quite incapable of taking any more. Not so with Chestnut – he never seemed to be satisfed and we had to be sure not to overfeed him; after 11 millilitres of the Lactol mixture we stopped offering any more. In the wild very young mammals are stimulated by their mothers to urinate and defecate. Without this stimulation there would be a build-up of the body's waste products causing inflation of the bladder and consequent poisoning. We tried

Chestnut reached up with both front paws.

to emulate the mother by using a damp tissue but luckily Chestnut was old enough not to need stimulation, in fact we had to take hasty evasive action to avoid his soaking us after every feed.

We had arranged a hospital cage heated to 25 Centigrade to keep him warm and avoid further shock. He snuggled right down into a bed of fresh tissue until only the top of his tail could be seen. However any noise whatsoever would prompt a little pointed face to peer out from the confines of his bed – he was not going to miss anything.

Our vet did call that evening and on checking Chestnut over remarked that the wounds were very similar to cat bites inflicted when two cats fought over territory. While I held the squirrel very tightly he gently pulled at the fur above its tail: amazingly a large patch of skin just came away revealing the whole of Chestnut's rump as a sore septic wound many times larger than we originally thought. The infection had spread right across his back, no wonder he could not use his tail, the whole of his rump was covered with deep septic holes, too deep to be animal bites. Could they be the result of an attack by a large owl, possibly a tawny? Most of our casualties are directly attributable to man yet it looked as though Chestnut was the victim of a completely natural incident. How he escaped the tawny owl we shall never know but his fighting spirit stood him in good stead as over the next few weeks we regularly subjected him to the treatment and dressing of his wounds.

The first treatment of the exposed area was as traumatic for me as it was for Chestnut. The infected flesh had to be cleaned with Savlon but it must have been agony for him as he was too young for any of the pain-killing drugs. As I dabbed with the cotton wool he somehow wriggled his head from under the towel, turned and sank his teeth into my finger. I can still feel the impact as his incisors struck bone. At times like this it's instinctive to shake an animal off but this would destroy any confidence the animal had in you. He did not realize that I was trying to help him, all he knew was that I was hurting him and aggravating an already very sore area. So, getting a firmer grip on his head, I pressed on with the essential cleaning of his wounds until with a dusting of antibiotic powder I had finished and could pay some attention to my bleeding finger. Sue bathed and plastered it with a dressing of magnesium sulphate paste to draw out any infection. I felt just like Chestnut but hope I was more amenable as my wounds were cleaned and dressed.

The following morning found Chestnut quite bright-eyed and perky. His wounds had dried nicely, all he would need this morning was a light cleaning and dressing of the sore area and a further antibiotic injection. Once this was out of the way he settled to another 11 millilitres of Lactol and was introduced to his first solid food, sliced boiled carrot. Squirrels usually sit most attractively on their haunches holding their food in their front paws but because of his sore rump Chestnut could not manage a squirrel-pose, he could only crouch on all fours nibbling the edges of the carrot just like any other rodent. He was obviously nearly weaned; it would only be a few days before we could stop the bottle-feeding altogether but for now it helped cement the bond between us giving him comfort and a feeling of security.

Keeping Chestnut's wounds uncovered had the desired effect; three days later there was a definite sign of healing with the flesh showing pink and healthy. However, my squirrel-bitten finger was deteriorating; it had swollen out of all proportion and the tell-tale red streak had started up my arm. Although I take great care to keep my anti-tetanus inoculations up to date there is no way of preventing the spread of infection from an animal bite. I knew then how Chestnut felt as a charming nurse at Stoke Mandeville Hospital subjected me to a very undignified injection of antibiotic. As always I seemed to suffer the blunt needle but situations like this do serve to stress the concentration needed when handling wild animals.

With the constant handling and wound-cleaning Chestnut unfortunately became very tame. Our intention at the hospital is never to get too familiar with any patient. We endeavour to release into the wild every creature taken in. To release a tamed animal is to condemn it to an untimely end at the hands of men or their dogs. We had no alternative than to keep Chestnut as a permanent resident and to let him become part of the family. As grey squirrels are classified as vermin it is against the law to keep one in captivity unless a permit is obtained from the Ministry of Agriculture. Explaining how we showed Chestnut to visiting schoolchildren, learning about the countryside, persuaded the Ministry to grant us a permit provided that we ensured that Chestnut was never let into the wild.

As it turned out Chestnut's injured leg never functioned properly again, the original wounds must have so damaged the muscles and tendons that full mobility could never be attained. He learnt to run and climb quite expertly but that leg impaired his progress making him much slower than a fit squirrel. In the wild he would have needed to vie with other male squirrels and could have been seriously injured by them. We treated another squirrel by fixing a stainless steel pin to hold a break in his femur, yet he was still far more agile than poor old Chestnut.

I am sure that the company of our family dog, Poppy, helped Chestnut overcome his initial shyness. She took to Chestnut and they became close friends, playing and sleeping together; Poppy was even allowed to steal some of his peanuts and Digestive biscuits. During his period of treatment Chestnut lived in a huge parrot cage perched on a wooden cabinet in a corner of our lounge. A long bough set across the cage led to his sleeping quarters, a wooden box fixed to the side of the cage and stuffed full of hay, paper and old woolly sweaters. As comfortable as he was Chestnut still preferred to be out and about the house. As soon as anybody entered the room he would

Poppy and Chestnut became close friends.

limp down and rattle the cage door until somebody let him out.

As he grew stronger and more confident he would extend his repertoire of antics culminating in a swift ascent of the lounge curtains, peering at us over the curtain rail first at one end then at the other. Even with the impediment of a damaged leg he never once fell although we were often very worried for his safety. We do receive injured squirrels that have fallen from trees, probably the result of skirmishes with other animals.

Chestnut was also very adept at climbing up visitors, perching prettily on their shoulders and gently nibbling their ears. I would never trust a wild animal completely and always disappointed people by removing Chestnut in case he became a little too boisterous. This did happen with Poppy; one minute they were playing as always, but one of Chestnut's nips must have been too strong for in a flurry of fur and snarls the sweet little harmless dog had Chestnut pinned by his neck to the floor. This time I rescued Chestnut from further damage but received another squirrel bite for my trouble. I cannot really blame him for this as I believe it was only a retaliatory action spurred by his ominous predicament in the jaws of Poppy. Holding him around his shoulders so that he could note bite again I tried to console him but his chattering teeth warned me that he was either angry or frightened. I did not want to inflame the situation so put him back in his cage where he sat defiantly cursing at Poppy. Then once again I had a moment to try and stem the flow of blood from my battered fingers. People often wonder why I advocate that squirrels do not make good pets; counting the scars on my hands gives justification to my argument. Sadly after that incident Poppy and Chestnut could never be trusted together again but I must add that Chestnut has only bitten me once since then. On that occasion I was rescuing a voluntary helper who had ignored my warning and had picked up Chestnut. He was badly bitten. I have known Chestnut for over three years but I will never take liberties with him as I know how obstinate squirrels can be. Using peanuts and other treats I always manage to coax him to do what I want. So far he has obliged.

Now that Chestnut could no longer be allowed the freedom of the house I had to design and build him an outside pen where he could run in surroundings as near to a woodland setting as I could create. Squirrels, being rodents, have enormous gnawing power. Their four incisor teeth continue growing throughout their lives forcing the animals to gnaw constantly on any suitable material; in the case of squirrels it is old trees and branches that serve the purpose. However it is now being proved that living trees are only attacked between May and July by grey squirrels seeking the salt-rich vascular system situated just under the bark on deciduous trees, their preferred target.

In extreme cases these constantly growing teeth can cause serious problems for the rodent. We have a rabbit that was brought in close to starvation. His incisor teeth did not meet when he clenched his jaw, consequently he could not wear them down and they had grown out of his mouth and were over $1\frac{1}{2}$ inches long, effectively preventing him from feeding. It's a simple and painless task for me to keep his teeth clipped to length but as this has to be carried out every week, sadly we cannot release him back into the wild.

Chestnut's teeth were perfect; I knew that he could easily gnaw his way out of one of our standard animal pens so I would have to build impregnability into his new house. A roll of heavy 16-gauge weld-mesh would thwart his efforts to gnaw his way out and fixing the supporting timbers outside the wire would protect them from damage. A double door hatch system prevented his darting out as you entered the pen, the outer door had to be closed before the inner door could be opened. A large tea chest, panelled and waterproofed, was fitted high under a roofed section. Filled with hay and old clothes it would make an ideal penthouse in which he could live and store his peanuts and other titbits. A mixture of hardy shrubs and a virtual Big Dipper of intercrossed heavy tree branches completed the construction. The pen was now ready for its pampered tenant.

Chestnut's parrot cage was too large to pass through the double door system into the pen so I had to carry him in. As I have said, it is unwise to pick Chestnut up but by offering him a favourite nut I coaxed him onto my shoulder for the short journey into the pen. He was concentrating on storing the chestnut inside my collar and did

Craftily I had put more chestnuts on a tall stump.

not seem to notice the transition into his new home. By the time I felt
the cold chestnut slip inside my shirt we were in. Craftily I had put
more chestnuts on a tall stump just under his new sleeping quarters.
Accepting my arm as a ladder he quickly ran to the feast but by the
time he had turned, intent on planting another nut in my collar, I
had managed to slip out unnoticed, leaving him to explore on his
own.

He loved his new-found freedom, scampering first up one branch, sniffing another, running circles on the ground, running up to me at the wire somehow imparting his excitement to me. However all the time that back leg was held stiffly to one side. I was pleased he liked his new home, as there was obviously no way he could survive in the wild. Then he found his new penthouse. First nervously sniffing the entrance, he took a few tentative steps inside but I had put some of his old bedding in there so the scent was familiar and in he went. There was much moving of hay and bedding until it was to his liking; squirrels do like their comfort. Satisfied for the moment, he poked his head out, did another high-speed circuit of the pen, collected a chestnut and made a big display of burying it in a dark corner of his box. A few more circuits chestnut-collecting, then he was tired. Retiring, he once more moved all the bedding round and then settled, happy with his new surroundings.

Squirrels are branded vermin by foresters yet enquiries have shown that they are in the Top Ten of the World's most popular animals, rubbing shoulders with giant pandas, koala bears, chimpanzees and other exotic animals. I know that whenever we show a school party over the hospital it is always Chestnut that they love to see. Of course he obliges by coming to the wire to greet them, showing off by hanging upside down to crack open the pine nuts that I let the children give him. The mesh on his pen is too small to let him even nibble an unwary finger but I must admit to being apprehensive every time he takes a nut.

Chestnut blossomed in his new surroundings, he grew a new coat to cover his massive scars and even learnt to compensate for his damaged leg. He looked superb and was much in demand for newspaper and television appearances encouraging people to support the work of the hospital but, as unpredictable as always, he blotted his copybook with one television crew. This particular appearance was to the music of Bright Eyes, the title of our magazine and the haunting theme of the motion picture *Watership Down*. He was performing beautifully in front of the cameras but in spite of our warnings one of the sound men picked him up. In went those teeth and the next ten minutes were spent trying to stop the bleeding.

The final straw was more out of mischief than spite and involved

Chestnut decided to liven up proceedings.

Bambi the fallow deer. I had allowed Chestnut the freedom of the garden while Bambi sat on the grass idly chewing the cud. Barry Keen, the chief photographer of the *Bucks Herald*, was using up film after film recording the squirrel's antics when suddenly Chestnut decided to join Bambi on the grass. He ran along Bambi's back, and all looked very peaceful and Barry captured some wonderful photographs. Then Chestnut decided to liven up the proceedings and nipped Bambi's ear. The deer went one way, the squirrel went the other and another animal friendship was over. Back Chestnut had to go into his pen, and I knew that never again could I trust him with any of the other patients.

As there is always plenty of activity at the hospital I do not believe that he feels his solitude and I must admit to spending more time than I can spare in his company. Perhaps one day a female squirrel will come along to fill his life.

9

How the White Owl Returned to London

In the early days of the hospital, before we had today's constant influx of casualties, Sue and I could leave a volunteer to do the feeding and reception while we took occasional weekend breaks at Swanage in Dorset. We got to know the countryside around Swanage, often noticing the number of derelict buildings and trees that would make perfect barn owl nesting or roosting sites. The barn owl is one of Britain's most elusive birds, and it is most bird-lovers' dream just to see one so, in 1981, we set aside a complete weekend with the sole purpose of tracking one down. A derelict barn on the hills above Swanage yielded feather and pellet evidence of barn owl occupation but the site now appeared vacant. Most of the weekend was spent on fruitless searches across the downs but eventually we spotted one lone bird quartering, like a giant butterfly, the wastes of the local council refuse tip. Obviously a good hunting area for rats, mice and voles. The sheer beauty of that ghostly flight resolved me to try in any way possible to save the barn owl from its impending extinction in Britain.

Still buzzing with that image, we made our way home to Aylesbury. The plans we made during that long drive seemed completely impossible but as always fate seemed to take a hand. About ten o'clock on the Sunday evening I had just turned onto a short cut about ten miles from Aylesbury when I noticed a light brown huddle in the middle of the road. Screeching to a halt I threw the car across the road to prevent oncoming traffic flattening what I thought was a rabbit. Running from the car I scooped the casualty up but found,

The Prodigal recovered well.

not the handful of fur I expected, but a bundle of soft feathers, a barn owl. Scarcely daring to dawdle any longer on the carriageway I ran back to the car, and, dumping my precious bundle on the back seat, I sped off towards Aylesbury, leaving the rest of the traffic to wonder about my sanity. Not a murmur from the recumbent owl, who was either heavily concussed or else very dead.

Back home at the hospital, Sue did the rounds of the new admissions while I dared to check the barn owl. He was breathing but showed no other signs of life. My manhandling caused him to half open one eye, the other remained closed. One explanation was that he was the victim of a hit-and-run driver but thankfully was only suffering from a slight concussion. Owls have a very thick covering of feathers over a very meagre body and I am sure that this padding saves many of them, especially tawny owls, from serious injury in their frequent collisions with motor vehicles. He was lucky, a night under an infra red lamp should see him greatly improved.

As I entered the intensive care unit the following morning, he flew at the bars of his cage, talons outstretched, whooshing all manner of barn owl defiance at me. He had recovered well but perhaps still had a lingering headache – his irascibility suggested so. I try to release casualties as soon as possible so as not to interrupt any pairing arrangements they might have in their territory, but I decided to keep him one more day to make sure that he did not slip back into unconsciousness and no doubt he relished the frozen mice served on demand. Dr Philip Burton came over and ringed the owl with a British Trust for Ornithology ring. The ring was numbered and marked 'Please inform the British Museum if found', which would let us know if anything disastrous happened to the bird after its release. Naturally we do not like to hear of recoveries as it usually means that the bird has died. We have had very few rings recovered, which indicates that our release programmes, for all species of birds, are working and that rehabilitated birds do, in the main, survive their return to the wild.

He looked a much livelier barn owl when I took him at dusk to where I had found him three days before. To give him the best chance of survival I travelled about two miles from the main road before releasing him into the gloom. He flew off strongly, dipping and floating as only barn owls can. I watched him disappear then turned for home.

One week later a late-night telephone call told of another barn owl road victim. Richard Duggan, a photographer on the *Bucks Herald*, had come across an unconscious barn owl in the middle of the road. He was bringing it straight to us. Twenty minutes later he arrived with the casualty wrapped in a sweater. As he recounted the story of its rescue I began to wonder: he had found it on the same stretch of road, in the same circumstances and had shown the same bravado in the face of oncoming traffic as I had done on my way back from Swanage nine days before. This barn owl had a ring on its leg. Yes, it was the same gleaming new ring. Once again the Prodigal had survived with just a mild concussion but we did not dare release him there again; the next time his padding of feathers might not save him.

Richard Duggan with the Prodigal.

We Save Wildlife

Like the good photographer he is, Richard had his cameras to hand giving me the delightful opportunity of reversing the normal role by putting him in front of the camera, a change he did not relish. How his colleagues must have ribbed him as the Prodigal's story was published in the *Bucks Herald* and Richard's photograph was displayed in hundreds of newsagents throughout the county.

The problem was where to release the Prodigal so that we could monitor his progress and recover him if he was in difficulty. Strangely our answer came in the shape of another barn owl casualty, this time a young female found injured on the fast dual carriageway into Amersham. We knew of a closely guarded nest site close to that road, and thought that our new patient had perhaps just left the nest, maybe on her maiden flight. This owl had a broken wing. If that could be repaired, possibly the pair of barn owls could be released together using the wired-off barn technique advocated by some barn owl enthusiasts.

However I knew the pitfalls that occur when trying to repair a bird's wing. I really could not contemplate a release until after I had seen how the wing healed, if it did heal.

Feeling gently along the wing I could detect that the two pieces of broken bone were grating as they touched but thankfully the jagged ends had not penetrated the skin which can allow infection to infiltrate and seriously hinder the chances of a satisfactory repair. I pulled the two broken pieces of the bone into line and used a simple cardboard splint made from a Weetabix packet, heavily taped with zinc-oxide plaster, which would immobilize the wing for the three weeks necessary for it to heal.

At first Mrs Barnes found it difficult to balance with the added weight to her immobilized wing but over the next twenty-four hours she learned to compensate and could stand normally. I introduced her to the Prodigal not knowing what to expect but I was ready to pull her out if there was any aggressive behaviour. As it was they merely stood together shoulder to shoulder, completely ignoring the hubbub of the hospital all around them. When they stood that close together it was easy to see the difference between the sexes; he had pure white breast feathers, whereas Mrs Barnes had a liberal sprinkling of dark speckles on hers. She also had a much darker line forming the frill that masks a barn owl's face.

Although barn owls will venture out during the day this happy couple made no attempt to move around except if I were to enter the domain of their aviary. The Prodigal, ever on the defensive, seemed to take great pleasure in flying past me and at an opportune moment sticking out a talon in the hope of catching me unaware. Only once did he manage to hook the end of my nose; it smarted for days, a painful reminder of one lapse of concentration. After that incident I took the added precaution of always wearing a glove in order to fend off any attack by those needle-sharp talons.

Over the next three weeks their aviary was a picture of domestic bliss, no arguing and fair sharing of the nightly rations of frozen mice. I knew that now I had to shatter this tranquillity as Mrs Barnes's splint had to be taken off. I tried to enter the aviary unnoticed, managing to reach the box before the Prodigal came out, hissing defiance at my intrusion. Fending him off with one gloved hand, I reached in and grabbed Mrs Barnes, then made a very rapid exit from the aviary, slamming the door in his face as once more he came in for an attack. In the surgery I cut away the plaster and cardboard cover of her wing. I tried to avoid damaging the feathers any more than necessary as it would take some time for her to grow fresh plumage. Flexing the injured bone between my fingers I could feel that it was now rigid with very little callousing formed, a good sign if she was to fly again. There was a great possibility that after a few week's exercising she would be able to join her mate in his dive-bombing attacks on any intruder, which usually meant me.

While she was recuperating we set about organizing a barn from which we could arrange the release of the two birds. Many farmers regret the disappearance of barn owls and have contacted us to offer their land as possible release sites. As a single pair of barn owls will catch over three thousand mice and rats annually, it's not difficult to see the benefit of a resident pair especially near grain stocks plagued with rodents. What we needed was an old wooden barn well away from the hazards of roads and egg-collectors. Our quest revealed the ideal situation, an old barn just outside Tring on the border of

We Save Wildlife

Hertfordshire. The lady farmer was thrilled at the possibility of having owls around her farm buildings and promised us all the help we needed to set the scheme in motion.

The easiest part of the barn to enclose was walled on three sides and only required wire-mesh to cover the open section. The back wall had a stout door that we could use as an entrance or, with the Prodigal in residence, as a hasty escape route. The lady farmer filled the open section with one-inch chicken mesh effectively making an aviary thirty feet long by twelve feet wide. The roof was sound and sloped from about seven feet high at the open section to over twenty feet high along the back wall. About halfway up the back wall, in the darkest corner, a partially enclosed tea chest was mounted that would serve as a nest box and a retreat from the light of the day. Should the pair of barn owls adapt to these new surroundings and should they start raising a family then the wire mesh would be opened so that they could come and go as they pleased. The draw of having young chicks in the nest should encourage them to return with any prey they should catch. The young would then be raised by free-flying parents and would eventually be able to join the adults on their nightly forays into the countryside. Once the youngsters became independent and dispersed then the adults would, we hoped, remain on the now open site to breed again the following year.

With much hissing and clawing, the Prodigal and Mrs Barnes were put into the tea chest nest box in the barn. Both promptly shot out, and, clattering to the wire mesh, they flew up and down the enclosure, forcing me to duck their outstretched talons. Mrs Barnes showed no trace of the injury that had threatened to debilitate her, she was as manoeuvrably lethal as her spouse. I put a dozen frozen mice onto the apron of their nest box and hastily retreated through the door in the wall, leaving them to reconnoitre and settle in their new home.

The following day I visited the barn and found Mrs Barnes inside the box with the Prodigal snoozing peacefully on top of it; he had not heard me come in. So far so good; from now on visits would be kept to a minimum. Our very helpful lady farmer would go in each day to remove uneaten food and put out fresh mice. It was now February, but we did hope they might start to breed this spring.

Possibly the six or seven weeks they were together at the hospital had cemented a bond between them, for early in March Mrs Barnes seemed reluctant to leave the nest box and did not even venture out to join the Prodigal on one of my infrequent visits to the barn. I thought that she might be sitting on eggs but I had to make sure she was not sitting low because of illness. Climbing up a rickety old ladder, I could see her in the torchlight squatting in the darkness at the back of the box. Needless to say she hissed vehemently but as she stood and swayed from side to side I could detect two gleaming white eggs underneath her. I nearly fell off the ladder but, satisfied she was all right, I left the barn; we had to be doubly careful now as any undue disturbance might make her desert the eggs. From now on the food would be taken into her by the Prodigal, she alone would incubate the eggs.

As barn owl eggs are laid at two-day intervals we could estimate that she had been sitting for about four days, leaving approximately another thirty days before they hatched. Even then we must not look into the box to see if an egg had hatched; if disturbed, barn owls have the reputation of eating their young, so we would have to wait at least another six weeks before any chicks would be of a reasonably safe size. As the weeks passed the Prodigal continued taking food to her, then on the twenty-eighth day she was up and about and very excited. Something was definitely happening in the box but there was no way we could find out what it was. At least one egg must have hatched for over the next weeks we could see food being taken into the nursery.

Six weeks passed since the probable hatching. We now had to know the situation in the nursery so that we could arrange to let the adults out before any young could fly. Slowly climbing the ladder with one gloved hand over my head to protect me from both adult birds, who were now getting very excited by my intrusion, I peered over the edge of the nest box into the darkness of the nursery. Swinging my torch from side to side I hoped to see at least one young barn owl with the usual oversize beak and feet that make these chicks so unattractive. Instead I was hissed at by two large balls of white fluff. Mrs Barnes had managed to hatch two youngsters who were now in the stage of growing their first flight feathers. I could clearly see the light-brown speckled primaries on the larger of the chicks. They had now outgrown the ugly stage of their early development and were beginning to look like barn owls. In less than three weeks they would be making their maiden flights, and there was no time to lose in opening up the wire mesh.

I arranged for the chicks to be ringed with BTO rings, and the next day went once more into the barn to lift the birds out for the ringer – but they were gone, no sign of them anywhere. Braving the attention of the two adult birds we searched every corner of the barn, no young barn owls. Somebody must have entered the barn in our absence and taken the chicks, no doubt to subject them to a life in captivity. However in order to keep a barn owl legally in a cage it must have a close ring put on one leg in the first few days after it hatched. Close rings are unbroken bands of aluminium made to fit the legs of specific species of bird. As the bird's foot starts to grow it then becomes impossible to slide the ring onto the leg. Only a few species of British birds are allowed to be kept in captivity; as the close ring cannot be put onto a bird older than a few days, the system ensures that wild birds are not illegally caught for the pet trade. As all our birds are eventually released we do not close ring any progeny, and stolen birds cannot legally be kept in captivity. In spite of all my efforts, I never did find out what had happened to those birds. I only hope that in time they managed to escape as I could not bear to think of them being cooped up for the rest of their lives.

The whole purpose of the wired-in barn project had been destroyed; without the young to attract them back the adult birds would probably fly off to a doubtful future, but as they were wild birds we had no alternative other than just to let them go. They might adopt the barn as home. At least then we could make sure that food was available if they did run into difficulties. As it was for a few days after the wire mesh was lifted, the barn owls flew around the farm, then they were gone; perhaps they had enough sense to resent the loss of their chicks. Who knows? We have never had a recovery of one of their rings, and hope they are still alive and together.

From the dearth of barn owls we experienced before we started the scheme, there now seemed to be an influx of birds especially from people who had captive barn owls but could not tolerate their incarceration any longer. From all over the country people contacted us asking if we could include their barn owl in a release scheme. There was one major problem with captive birds; if they were permanently imprinted on humans they would not hesitate, after any release, to fly to the first person they saw. Even unintentionally, a barn owl's talons can cause nasty wounds and of course there are still those people who would not hesitate to capture an approaching barn owl or even to shoot at it although both activities are completely illegal. We had to turn away imprinted birds for their own sake but of the others that were offered there was one particular female who seemed ideal for inclusion in a release programme. She had been kept in a large cage standing in a pet shop in North London. Although the bird, having been cage bred and close ringed, was legally in captivity its owner dearly wanted it to have a chance of flying freely in the open night sky. It showed no signs of tameness and I was assured that it regularly caught mice as they passed through its cage so it was quite able to hunt in the wild.

Another young male had been hand raised from being found abandoned as a chick. He was quite unaffected by his experiences and was loath to be approached by anybody. My entry into his aviary was greeted with the usual vehement hissing and if I approached any closer he would flip onto his back, striking viciously with his talons – quite a formidable character. He had the clear white chest of a typical male but after only a week at the hospital he presented us with an egg. See how difficult it is to sex barn owls.

We now had two females suitable for release but needed a male to complete the trio, which would give more guarantee of breeding at the next release site. We received many telephone calls about injured barn owls but on arrival at the hospital they were either tawny or little owls. These all received the best of attention and were eventually released in various locations, they did not need the specialized release schemes demanded by barn owls.

We Save Wildlife

At last a male barn owl was picked up on the other side of High Wycombe. He had suffered only minor abrasions to his wing, possibly he had collided with overhead wires, an increasing source of danger to flying birds. From his plumage I estimated that he was immature and unlikely to be already involved in breeding. If he had been a mature male, possibly with a mate in the area, I would have endeavoured to return him to the place where he was found. This male was obviously a bachelor and so perfect for introduction to our two females. We had the trio; now to find a suitable barn.

The Wildlife Hospitals Trust, a registered charity, survives purely on voluntary donations and fundraising. Each year as part of the fundraising programme we set up a display and stall at the Greater London Council's educational farm at Harefield on the outskirts of the capital. The GLC has two working farms at Harefield covering a considerable acreage of protected land scattered with all manner of timber buildings that could be ideal for barn owls. As barn owls had not been seen wild in London for over ten years, this seemed the perfect opportunity both to release the three owls and to introduce them to a potentially bounteous feeding area. We discussed the idea with Illtyd Harrington, the Chairman of the GLC, when we met him at the farm's open weekend. Being dedicated to the conservation of London's wildlife, he put the wheels in motion and called up all the GLC's resources to make the release programme possible. Malcolm Francis, the GLC man on the spot, suggested a suitable old timber-framed barn that we could use. He also arranged the supply of wire mesh and timber necessary to enclose a section of the barn and provided the very important freezer in which we could store the frozen mice. One of the trust's members, Mark Morgan, lived near the farm and had great experience as a licensed BTO ringer of birds in that area. Mark was familiar with the barn and was quite willing to organize a team for wiring off the chosen section and for feeding the birds every day until their eventual independence.

One weekend's hectic activity saw the owl section completed with a partially enclosed tea chest mounted on a beam. My strongest proviso was that a padlock be fitted to the door for, although the location was a closely guarded secret, I still remembered that empty

The male barn owl and a female entered the barn at Harefield.

nest box on the first site, and since then all sites have been padlocked.

It was a very wet first day of February when we trudged through the mud to introduce the trio of barn owls to the darkness of the barn. They now had even more flying space and the small hatch feeding tray Mark had built made sure that they suffered the minimum of human intrusion.

Mark and his team arranged a rota for the daily feeding. For six or seven weeks the food was taken every day with occasionally all three birds putting in an appearance. Then towards the end of March Mark noticed that only two birds were now flying around the area. Not knowing what to expect, he climbed in and approached the nest box half expecting to come across a tragedy, but the missing female was sitting tightly on the floor. Braving her hacking beak he gently lifted her and there they were: six smooth white eggs, probably the first barn owl eggs laid in London for a quarter of a century. Mark beat a hasty retreat and could not wait to phone us at Aylesbury with the great news. Now all we could do was wait.

Knowing that barn owls incubate for thirty-two days, we could estimate that if the eggs were fertile they could hatch in the last two weeks of April. Mark and his team continued the feeding, only ever seeing the two owls, whilst the broody hen stayed with her eggs. By the beginning of May we assumed that any eggs had hatched but once again we did not dare investigate in case this mother ate her progeny. Gradually the numbers of mice taken increased from twelve each night to over twenty and then thirty; there were obviously healthy ravenous chicks in that box and judging by the increased consumption of food they must be growing at a fantastic rate. On the twentieth of May we decided to try and see into the box without disturbing the owls. From a safe distance, by torchlight we could just about make out the shadowy forms of three well grown chicks; we could not see into the far corners of the box so could not tell if there were any others. Once again we would just have to wait but we were all very excited at having seen at least three youngsters.

We had planned to disturb the owls only once, that was in order to put BTO rings on the chicks. Our D-Day was the fourth of June. The idea of seeing the young had attracted quite a gathering, including a television news crew, many, many newspapers and of course Mark and his team who would have the added bonus of ringing the barn owls, a rare opportunity that not many ringers experience. Not wanting to disturb the adult unnecessarily we decided to bring the youngsters out of the barn so that everybody could see them. They were tremendous, five of them, ranging from the largest with its glorious primary feathers already formed, to the smallest, a ball of white down blowing in the wind. It was like a Hollywood première, camera after camera clicked and whirred on but the owls were quite unconcerned, in fact dozing off when we wanted them awake. Quickly the rings were put on and recorded and the five chicks put back in the box. They would have two days to settle after this experience and then we would lift the wire and allow the adults their freedom.

Come the sixth of June, we lifted the wire from one of the barn

The young barn owls were tremendous — five of them.

entrances and waited, half expecting all three adults to disappear into the dusk, but no, they behaved as we had hoped and stayed loyal to the youngsters. In fact up to this moment, three days after the opening, not one barn owl has ventured out into the Harefield night. Once again all we can do is wait.

10

St Tiggywinkle's – Britain's First Hedgehog Hospital Unit

There is an ancient Anglo-Roman proverb which states, 'The fox has many tricks, the hedgehog only one and that greater than them all.' This ability to roll into an impregnable ball may have saved many hedgehogs in the Dark Ages but modern technology has severely limited its efficacy: today literally thousands of the harmless little insectivores are falling victim to motor cars, slug pellets, cattle grids and the new massive machinery that is cutting enormous swathes across Britain's countryside. At the moment we are looking after a mother hedgehog and her four babies that were accidentally scooped up in the massive jaws of a mechanical digger. Luckily the distressed driver had the presence of mind not to touch the youngsters with his bare hands, his human scent could have caused the mother to desert or – even worse – eat her progeny. Using thick gloves he carefully transferred the whole family to a cardboard box and raced them to us at St Tiggywinkle's.

Also using thick gloves, I transferred the five hedgehogs to a vacant pen where I could leave them undisturbed until the youngsters were no longer reliant on their mother's milk. Hedgehog mothers are notorious for deserting their young if they are disturbed and as this family had been carried halfway across Buckinghamshire I was seriously concerned for the welfare of the four mites who still did not even have their eyes open. I restricted anybody but me from

Four happy wrinkled pin-cushions with a very contented mother.

visiting the pen and every two hours checked on their progress. Each time I took my quick peek there were the four wrinkled pin-cushions happily suckling on a very contented mother. I now only check her once a day but am sure that the dangerous transition period is over.

It is now July and we are bursting at the seams with injured and baby hedgehogs. Thank goodness we now have St Tiggywinkle's and are able to offer all of them the best available facilities.

It was during the summer of 1984 that the serious plight of the hedgehog really struck home. The drought was decimating the numbers of newly born hedgehogs and dozens were being brought into us suffering from dehydration and other injuries received in their desperate search for food and moisture. We instigated massive newspaper and television appeals for people to put out extra water and moist cat and dog food for any visiting hedgehogs. People did care and, judging from the letters we received from all over the

Dozens of newly born hedgehogs were brought in to us.

country, many hedgehogs took advantage of these oases and no doubt many lives were saved.

However another major problem for hedgehogs was beginning to manifest itself; the new awareness of hedgehogs had caused people to look more closely at their night-time visitors and, horror upon horrors, many were seen to have injuries or serious disabilities. Of course we advised that they should be taken to local veterinarians but the message came back that many practices were unable or often unwilling to work on the casualties. We had many despairing calls from people who had found injured hedgehogs; many could not even persuade the animals to unroll and so could not judge the extent of any injuries, let alone attempt to treat them. We were quite willing to take in any of these casualties and our local veterinary practice, Tuckett, Gray and Partners, readily agreed to treat any beyond the resources of the hospital.

It's a question of time with hedgehogs: initially up to an hour can be spent gently rocking the animal, encouraging it to open up so that any fly damage can be treated with the anti-maggot powder Negasunt, any fly eggs picked off, and the extent of any injuries evaluated in order to plan a treatment. Patience is essential at this early stage, but some hedgehogs still refuse to uncurl and have to be referred to vets, who inject them with the muscle-relaxant Ketamine. Ten minutes after an injection even the most stubborn hedgehog will be stretched out ready for inspection. They suffer no after-effects of the Ketamine and are soon curled back into their impregnable balls.

Before long people from all over the country were bringing their hedgehog casualties to Aylesbury, many showing their deep concern by driving two or three hundred miles through the night so that the animal could get treatment as soon as was possible. Thump was one of the larger hedgehogs to arrive in the middle of the night. She had been driven all the way from Derbyshire and was obviously in need of attention; she even found it too painful to curl into a ball. The unnatural swelling of her abdomen suggested some internal damage and as her left front leg dangled hideously I could readily assume that there was a fracture or dislocation. These types of injuries in a mammal are too painful to treat without deep anaesthesia so until

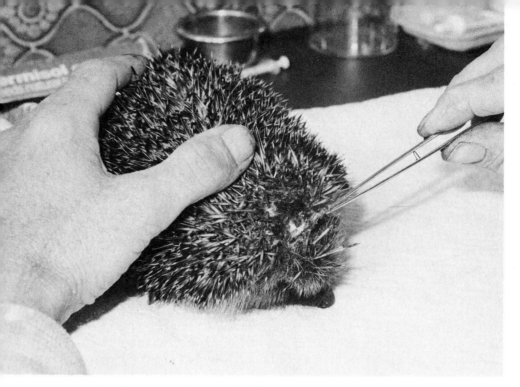

Any fly eggs can be picked off with tweezers.

morning I just offered her droppers of glucose and water to help alleviate her shock. Dribbling the fluid into her mouth I could not help noticing the excessive movement of her bottom jaw; this too looked like a fracture across the symphysis where the two bottom mandibles met at the front of the jaw.

The following morning Richard Hill, the veterinary surgeon who did most of our work, felt the swelling of the abdomen and diagnosed a probable rupture of the muscle wall surrounding the stomach, a condition needing immediate surgery. We were uncertain whether anybody had ever operated on a hedgehog before, but with Thump spreadeagled under halothane anaesthesia Richard started the operation. 'She is the same as a dog inside,' he declared as he sought out

(Opposite) *Thump having glucose after her operation.*

120

the tear in the muscle wall. Checking all over for other internal damage he was satisfied of only the one tear and dexterously stitched it together with absorbable cat-gut sutures. Pulling and stitching the covering skin together produced a nice round hedgehog again, without the horrible swelling that had caused so much concern. While Thump was unconscious Richard fixed the broken symphysis with surgical wire and encased the fractured leg in a rigid plaster cast. As Thump came round from the anaesthetic she found that she could now, somewhat painfully, nearly curl up but that plastered leg would not bend and remained sticking ridiculously out of the prickly ball. The treating of small wild animals with pain killers is a completely untested field of animal surgery, so rather than gamble with her life she would have to endure some soreness for just a few days.

Back at the Wildlife Hospital Thump would need a cage to herself to stop any other hedgehogs aggravating her healing wounds but all of the cages had resident casualties; we decided they would have to share. The well-being of a hedgehog can be judged by its appetite; with one animal per cage it was easy to see how it was eating but more than one could mean that a non-eater could be overlooked. Also hedgehogs have the nasty habit of chewing anything that remotely resembles meat and as this can include fellow hedgehogs, sharing could mean that a weak animal might not be able to escape the unwelcome attentions of a cage-mate. Sue and I had regularly discussed the merits of a specialized unit with cages and equipment designed to cater for the individuality of hedgehogs but as always the lack of funds prevented us proceeding further. We even dreamed of calling the unit St Tiggywinkle's after the Beatrix Potter character that did so much to endear hedgehogs to so many young people. For the moment, though, we had to fit Thump into an inside cage somewhere.

Luckily another of the hedgehog patients was ready to start his convalescence in an outdoor pen although he would have to be brought inside for the first few nights. His vacant cage would suit our latest arrival and, judging by the way she tucked into her first meal of puppy food, she found the quarters acceptable and the wire holding her jaw did not interfere with her feeding. She coped remarkably well with her plastered leg though looking at the state of the plaster I could swear that she used it to stir her puppy food. It was important to keep her stitches clean for the first few days so whilst cleaning I took the opportunity to check that the plaster on her leg was not too tight and hindering the blood circulation to her foot. After about a week her foot began to swell and look chafed where the plaster ended, but cutting away some of the plaster and lubricating the sore parts soon alleviated the problem.

Ten days after the operation Richard removed her stitches, the incision having healed beautifully. The wire was removed from her jaw after four weeks and the plaster cast from her leg two weeks later. It was hard to imagine that such a short time ago this robust bustling hedgehog could neither walk nor feed. Now she too could go outdoors to convalesce and would eventually be released in an enormous garden well away from the traffic hazards that had so nearly killed her.

The numbers of hedgehogs needing care rose steadily; we were never sure whether our present facilities could cope but somehow, by keeping to a regular convalescence and release programme, we always managed to give any casualty the best of attention. Just when it seemed that we would have to start keeping animals in the house, a regular supporter of the trust, Chris Dunkley, gave us the great news that he had been offered a chalet-style timber building for the hospital by Mr John Morley whose company, the Gatemakers, specialized in wooden buildings. The offer could not have come at a more appropriate moment, we would now be able to care for any number of hedgehogs who could have far more spacious accommodation than we had at the moment.

Mr Morley came and personally supervised the building's erection. When it was complete it would not only serve as a hedgehog and medical unit, but its style would grace the hospital complex for many years to come. I designed and built individual cages with removable fronts and trays that were easily cleaned. Each cage could be joined to its neighbour in order to take family groups or extra large adults. St Tiggywinkle's was ready for the next influx of

We Save Wildlife

casualties, but the very first hedgehog to arrive was nearly too large to fit even our new double cages. Chris Mead, the eminent ornithologist, had been handed an unfortunate hedgehog that had somehow been inflated, like a balloon, to the size of a football. Its skin had distended so much that its legs and feet projected sideways, quite unable to reach the ground.

Billy Bunter, as we called him, was full of some form of gas, but there were no obvious signs of what had caused this to happen. It could have been gangrenous in nature, so after we fitted a tap to a hypodermic needle and syringe and drew off the gas we put Billy on a course of antibiotics to try to prevent a recurrence of the problem. When he was fully deflated his skin, which had been so stretched, now hung around him like a prickly hovercraft skirt, it dragged on the floor as he regained his ability to walk. The skin would soon shrink to normal size and, judging by his appetite, he felt much better as he settled into the new five-star accommodation of a double

Billy Bunter was full of some form of gas.

cage at St Tiggywinkle's. He would have to stay under observation for a few weeks so we could see if the gas reappeared and also complete the course of antibiotics. Luckily it never did re-occur and Billy was eventually released.

The numbers of casualties increased as it became known that at last somebody was willing to try and save these hedgehogs, but we became more and more concerned that some people just did not have the facilities to make the long journey to Aylesbury. There did seem to be a simple solution: for many years pigeon fanciers and other animal groups had used British Rail's livestock carriage service that guaranteed to carry a bird from one station to another, anywhere in the United Kingdom, in under twenty-four hours. After an initial first aid a hedgehog could quite safely be transported to Aylesbury and as it was unlikely to suffer any ill effects on such a journey we could probably then save its life. British Rail readily consented to carry the hedgehogs and agreed to impose only the minimum charge on the service.

No sooner had the scheme been mentioned than the first hedgehog rail traveller was on its way to St Tiggywinkle's. Coming from Kingston in Surrey the young hedgehog arrived at Aylesbury Station within twelve hours of despatch. The staff at Aylesbury Station were as thrilled as we were at the first success but as Sue and I sped to collect the package we wondered at the condition of the casualty and how he had taken the journey. We need not have worried, for Casey seemed to have ignored the upheaval, he was warm and snug in his bed of hay as if nothing had happened. He had a slight wound on one leg, which was the reason he was sent, but apart from that he seemed quite fit. After a few day's bathing with Dermisol and hearty meals of puppy food he could be released as good as new.

The prognosis for all those injured hedgehogs looked good until red tape stopped the scheme. The British Rail Board had unearthed a clause in an old Government Transit of Animals Order which restricted the transport of any animal that was unfit. Particularly applicable to domestic cattle and sheep, the clause strove to prevent unnecessary suffering but I am sure that the civil servants who drew up the order did not realize that each spine on a hedgehog has a

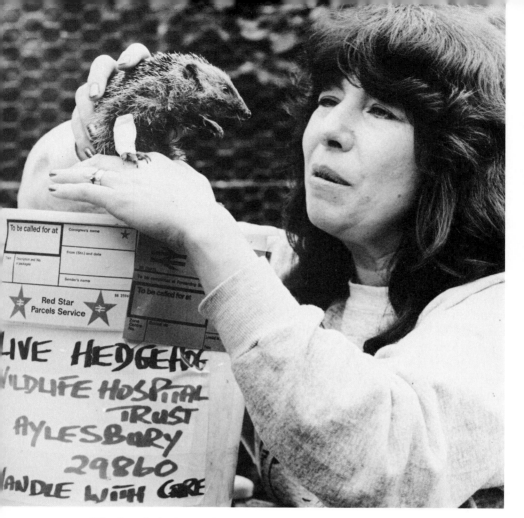

The first hedgehog rail traveller was on its way.

built-in shock absorber. Combined, these shock absorbers make a
very efficient barrier that protect a hedgehog even if it were,
hypothetically, to be sent by post. A hedgehog incurs no suffering
when transported by train and even if it did that would be preferable
to a slow, lingering, painful death, the inevitable result of untreated
injuries. But the board would not budge, although British Rail are
allowed to carry injured hedgehogs if the sender first obtains a

126

veterinary certificate. We are now back to the same impasse, with many vets refusing to have anything to do with hedgehogs. Robert Jones, a member of Parliament with strong feelings for wildlife, has been very helpful in trying to get hedgehogs exempted from the Transit of Animals Order and is still taking their case to the highest authorities. All this in spite of a visit to St Tiggywinkle's when Jaws, one of the patients, decided to bite his first MP. Luckily no blood was drawn and his voracity has not jeopardized the position of other needy patients. In the meantime kind people are still bringing casualties to St Tiggywinkle's and the occasional hedgehog slips through to Aylesbury Station disguised as a racing pigeon but somehow I cannot help thinking of all those that are suffering, untreated because of an obsolete law.

One of the casualties to overwinter with us was Blind Pew. He had suffered massive head injuries from being trapped under a bonfire but had finally been caught swimming in a pit of oil in a motor repair shop. Undaunted by his injuries and lack of sight Blind Pew responded to being cleaned up in washing-up liquid and, with his wounds healed, settled down to a pampered life as our only resident hedgehog having the freedom of the garden and nightly tin of cat food to sustain him. His sense of smell was phenomenal, he soon had a complete network of invisible paths to follow and would disappear into his lair in a trice if one of our dogs even ventured into his domain. His one drawback was that unsavoury hedgehog habit of chewing anything that resembled meat and one shattered night I was awoken by a frenzied quacking only to find one of our injured ducks paddling frantically round the garden with Pew hanging on to its tail as though it was the tastiest meal to pass his way in some time. The duck was penned from that moment on and Pew had the garden to himself. That was until this spring when a blind lady hedgehog, Jog, was brought into St Tiggywinkle's. Like Pew, she could not be released and was introduced into the garden. Pew sniffed, realized this was not food, then set off in a mad rush; round and round the garden he went at a furious rate. Then back to Jog, another sniff then off on another dozen or so circuits. Could this be hedgehog love? Jog started her circuits, though not as frantically as her beau. They have lived under St Tiggywinkle's for some months now and I believe, judging by the size of Jog, that they are expecting a happy event.

We now have considerable experience of many hedgehog problems although we are just touching the tip of the iceberg in researching their many debilitating internal parasites. The work at St Tiggywinkle's has just been chosen as an award winner by the Conservation Foundation, so this will enable us to take in and hopefully cure even more of these wonderful little animals.